THE MILITANT CHURCH

THE MILITANT CHURCH

LESTER SUMRALL

Whitaker House

THE MILITANT CHURCH

Lester Sumrall
Lester Sumrall Evangelistic Association, Inc.
P.O. Box 12
South Bend, IN 46624

ISBN: 0-88368-364-4
Printed in the United States of America
Copyright © 1995 by Whitaker House
Images © 1994 PhotoDisc, Inc.

Whitaker House
580 Pittsburgh Street
Springdale, PA 15144

1 2 3 4 5 6 7 8 9 10 11 / 05 04 03 02 01 00 99 98 97 96 95

Contents

Introduction

The world is on a collision course and doesn't know it. These are end-time days, but the world has no idea what lies ahead. All around us, in various pockets of the world, we hear of unrest, turmoil, fighting and famine. In other places, men and women are living life to the hilt, unconcerned about the homeless and hungry, drinking, partying, marrying, divorcing, remarrying, indulging in their homosexual liasons, seeking status...and on and on it goes.

Men think of the world as a playground. But militant Christians know otherwise. This world isn't a playground, it's a battleground. We're not here to fight, the world says, we are here to frolic. Sadly, even many Christians have adopted that attitude. Oh, they wouldn't say that in so many words, but their lifestyles and their conduct gives them away. Careless, carnal "Christianity."

You don't have to delve too far back into history to see that things are far different today than they were for our founding fathers and the early development of our country. There is a wide gulf between our attitudes and that of those forefathers. There was a time when Christianity exercised a dominant influence over American thinking. What made the difference?

These people knew the world was a battleground. They believed in sin, the devil, and hell as constituting one force; with God, righteousness, heaven and God's people as the other. They recognized that in this battle you can't be neutral. It's life or death, heaven or hell, and if a man is to come out on the winning side, he can expect to do war with God's enemies. The fight is real, long and deadly, and it lasts as long as life continues here below. Heaven is home where the soldier enjoys the peace God has prepared for those who love Him, who serve Him, and are faithful to the end. The end counts.

In heaven we won't need our armor. We can shed it as we enter its portals. There we will be given the victor's crown and robe of righteousness reserved for the stalwart (Rev. 6:11; 7:9-17).

But in the meantime, tremendous spiritual forces are present in the world, and we are caught in the middle. Evil powers are intent on destroying the godly; but arrayed against these demonic forces, are the heavenly hosts helping God's faithful people. This is war. It requires militancy on the part of Christians. This book is a call to those who name the Name of Christ to put on their armor and to advance against the devil. It is an urgent plea for Christians to recognize that this is war, to take up the sword of the Spirit, the Word of God, and to use it with Holy Spirit empowerment.

Lester Sumrall

1

No Summer Soldiers

In God's army, you cannot be just a summer soldier; full-time service is required. It comes with the territory. In the United States military, there is a place for short-time enlistees; but God's service is not like that.

God wants soldiers who are in it for the duration, soldiers who make a lifetime commitment to Him. From the moment you say yes to Jesus, you are in His service until you die — unless you go AWOL or shirk your duty.

Does that sound like a stiff sentence? It may, if you do not personally know the Commander-in-Chief.

Volunteers for service with the Lord will not find it to be just a holy huddle. Spiritual warfare is just as real as any shooting war on the earth. Soldiers without their armor or who do not use their weapons can get ambushed, wounded and even killed, just as in a natural battle. And today, perhaps more than at any other time in history, Satan's maneuvers are escalating. One look at your daily paper should convince you of this.

Those who have served in the military — regardless the branch of service — will tell you being in the armed service is serious business, even in peacetime. It's not games you play. From the moment you enter the army, navy, marines, or air force, you are a part of something that exacts a price. Discipline and strict obedience to orders are not only expected but required.

As Christians, we use military terms quite glibly sometimes in our reference to the warfare of the Christian life. Yet, far too often there is little real militancy, little willingness to endure, and a noticeable lack of a conquering spirit.

We understand so little about the Lord's battle plans. Make no mistake, living the Christian life means engaging in warfare when you are doing it God's way!

This Is a Time for Active Warfare

The Apostle Paul understood the language of militancy. In the Mediterranean world, the first century A.D., soldiers and military installations were commonplace. In many places throughout his letters, you find him referring to what it takes to be a good soldier. For instance, Paul, in writing to young Timothy, said, **You therefore must endure hardship as a good soldier of Jesus Christ** (2 Tim. 2:3).

Military men are trained and equipped to do battle against the enemy. Carrying that analogy over into the need for militancy in God's army — and keeping in mind what the apostle wrote — one is impressed with the fact that we are not to play at being soldiers. We are to take the idea of active spiritual warfare seriously.

The call for effective service carries with it an implied understanding that we are to do battle, using our weapons in advancing against the enemy. This is not peacetime soldiering! We are to be soldiers who know the battle plan and are mobilized for action.

We are called to be courageous in the face of satanic attacks. Those who truly love God will know what it means to face this adversary. Peter wrote that genuine faith will be tested by fire (1 Pet. 1:7), and he wrote of the need to be willing to suffer for righteousness' sake (1 Pet. 3:14).

He also warned of the need to be courageously vigilant, ever watchful:

> **Be sober, be vigilant; because your adversary the devil walks about like a roaring lion, seeking whom he may devour.**
>
> **Resist him, steadfast in the faith, knowing that the same sufferings are experienced by your brotherhood in the world.**
>
> **1 Peter 5:8,9**

Paul wrote his second letter to Timothy from a cold, damp, dark dungeon, a condemned criminal awaiting death. His crime? Faithfulness to the Lord. . . . **for I know whom I have believed** (2 Tim. 1:12), Paul wrote. He had staked his faith in Christ. Most of us will never suffer as the apostle suffered for his faith. (2 Tim. 1:8.) Some will never get close enough to hear the "lion" roar.

Where do you get the kind of courage Paul had? You get it from the Spirit of God who produces what it takes for you to do battle for the Lord.

Remember Joshua's charge to the people whom he was to lead into the Promised Land after the death of Moses? After telling them to meditate upon the Book of the Law and to do what it commanded, Joshua said:

> **"Have I not commanded you? Be strong and of
> good courage; do not be afraid, nor be dismayed, for
> the Lord your God is with you wherever you go."**
> **Joshua 1:9**

Militancy God's way comes as we know the Word of God and are faithful to what it says. There are disciplines involved in good soldiering. These include fortifying ourselves mentally and emotionally with that which will equip us to wage spiritual warfare.

In much of our prayerline counseling, our counselors frequently discover the reason for the depression, discouragement, and problems faced by the callers is that they are not staying close to the Word of God. The reason so many of the same people show up at the altar week after week in church services can very often be traced to their failure to know and apply the principles of the Word of God to their daily experiences and to their relationships.

Protection for Believers

The way to be strong and to walk in God's power is to have on the armor of Jesus. The Apostle Paul explains that the believers' enemies are the demonic hosts of Satan, assembled for mortal combat. Christians are the targets of Satan. We are to fight with truth, righteousness, peace, faith, salvation, the Word of God, and prayer. (Eph. 6:13-18.)

The world would regard this as strange weaponry. But Paul took the pieces of armor worn by Roman soldiers and made spiritual applications from them.

The Belt of Truth

Stand firm then, with the belt of truth buckled around your waist ....

Ephesians 6:14a NIV

Truth implies truthfulness. Where there is deceit and lying in the life of a believer, his falsehood forfeits the very thing that holds the other pieces of his armor together.

In the ancient garment of Paul's day, the girdle about the loins held in place every other part of the uniform of the soldier. If you want to know the facts, if the girdle (the belt) was lost, you lost everything! How embarrassing that could be! We've all seen comedy routines where the comic's trousers drooped down around his ankles, but that wouldn't be funny in battle. In fact, I read of a great battle in the past where the clever general told his men to cut the belts of the enemy troops while they were sleeping. When they awoke and got up the next morning, the men were so busy holding up their pants they weren't able to shoot their guns and lost the battle.

I don't know if that's really a true story, but the point is good. We are to be girded with truth in the face of the enemy. You never go wrong telling the right thing, the truthful thing.

The Breastplate of Righteousness

... with the breastplate of righteousness in place....

Ephesians 6:14b NIV

The breastplace was to protect the heart of the soldier. Unrighteous acts committed by a Christian rob him of this vital protection and expose his heart to Satan. Maintaining your breastplate of righteousness protects your heart.

Hebrews 10:22 teaches, **Let us draw near with a true heart in full assurance of faith, having our hearts sprinkled from an evil conscience and our bodies washed with pure water.**

Without a heart free from an evil conscience (seared, burdened with sin, hardened), you cannot have a heart established and strengthened by means of God's grace. **For it is good that the heart be established by grace ...** (Heb. 13:9).

James, chapter 1, teaches, **If anyone among you thinks he is religious, and does not bridle his tongue but deceives his own heart, this one's religion is useless** (vs. 26).

A person does not secure God's grace until he abandons his sinful ways and walks in integrity. An immoral lifestyle does not secure God's grace. You can't have sin in your life and expect to wage warfare with the enemy.

Christ is our righteousness. The filthy rags of self-righteousness are useless as a breastplate. There has to be a heart and a conscience that are right with God.

Feet Fitted With the Gospel of Peace

> ... and with your feet fitted with the readiness
> that comes from the gospel of peace.
>
> **Ephesians 6:15** NIV

This implies firm-footed stability in times of attack. Romans wore sandals which were bound by thongs over the instep and around the ankle, and the soles were studded thickly with nails. This is the picture the Apostle Paul presents.

Shoes speak of a foundation for our feet, something that will keep us from slipping and sliding. Christ is our rock, our foundation. **For no other foundation can anyone lay than that which is laid, which is Jesus Christ** (1 Cor. 3:11).

We are not to be as mere mercenaries thrust into battle, but we are to be committed volunteers who made a choice, heard the higher call and enlisted our very lives under the service of the Prince of Peace. We feel driven into warfare with the gospel that brings everlasting peace. We seek aggressively to take the message into the fear-ridden human battleground. We do not fear the combat zone. We are ready to declare war to bring peace. We seek to end the strife between man and God. While we are militant men and women, yet we are peacemakers. **Blessed are the peacemakers, For they shall be called sons of God** (Matt. 5:9).

The Shield of Faith

In addition to all this, take up the shield of faith, with which you can extinguish all the flaming arrows of the evil one.

Ephesians 6:16 NIV

The *shield* of the heavy infantry was a large, oblong piece of metal, curved on the inner sides. There is no better description of how this faith shield was used by great biblical saints than that which can be found in Hebrews 11, often called "the catalog of faith" chapter.

To many people, faith is a leap in the dark, an uncertainty, some kind of gamble. I protest that! Others say faith is a great mystery. I have found faith to be a force moving deep down in my spirit. Faith to change the world is an inner force — a power beyond ourselves. The writer of Hebrews tells us that **faith is the substance of things hoped for, the evidence of things not seen** (Heb. 11:1).

Substance? What does that mean? It's been described as "the title deed," meaning the Word of God, resting upon what God says, believing God. Faith is not just historical, although Hebrews 11 provides historical data relative to the faith of Abel, Enoch, Noah, Abraham and Sarah, Isaac, Jacob, Joseph, Moses, and "others;" but faith *is!* It's right now. Faith functions; faith moves mountains — now.

To build an Empire-State-Building-kind of faith, you must put your footings deep. The devil will knock you off your faith if you have little sand footings. The two colossal faith footings which cannot be moved by earthquakes, the devil, or anything are these: (1) Know there is a God; and (2) Know that He is a rewarder of those who diligently seek Him. (Heb. 11:6.)

You get to know people by spending time with them. Just so, you get to know God and your faith deepens as you spend time with Him in His Word.

People eulogize Smith Wigglesworth calling him a prophet of faith. But what they don't know is how much time he spent in the Word of God. I got to know Smith Wigglesworth real well by spending a lot of time with him, but in the process, I got to know the God he loved and served much better because we'd spend hours together in the Bible. No wonder things happened in his ministry. He knew God exists. He had strong faith. He knew how to take up the shield of faith and use it to extinguish the flaming arrows of the evil one.

The Helmet of Salvation

Take the helmet of salvation....

Ephesians 6:17 NIV

The *helmet of salvation* refers to protection for the head and the brain. Surely it implies understanding and knowledge gleaned from reading the Bible so that one's eyes are not blinded, ears deafened, or the mind confused with attacks from the world, the flesh, and the devil.

God does appeal to the mind of man, to the intellect as well as to his spirit. So that's why it is essential that we protect the head. In another of his letters the Apostle Paul mentions this piece of armor: **But let us who are of the day be sober, putting on the breastplate of faith and love, and as a helmet the hope of salvation** (1 Thess. 5:8).

In three places in Ephesians 6, we are told that having on these pieces of armor will enable us to stand in militant warfare. **Put on the whole armor of God, that you may be able to stand against the wiles of the devil** (v. 11; see also vv. 13,14).

The Sword of the Spirit

... and the sword of the Spirit, which is the word of God.

Ephesians 6:17b NIV

The apostle now switches from defensive weaponry to offensive. All the pieces of armor mentioned thus far have been for defense — everything is for the front of the individual. This says to me that we are not to be retreating Christians, but advancing soldiers waging spiritual warfare. But in Ephesians 6:17b, Paul tells us we will need a sword, but not just any old weapon in our hand. We are to wield **the sword of the Spirit, which is the Word of God,** and this is a weapon of offense.

Hebrews 4:12 tells us about that weapon. **For the word of God is living and powerful, and sharper than any two-edged sword, piercing even to the division of soul and spirit, and of joints and marrow, and is a discerner of the thoughts and intents of the heart.**

Once again, Paul is pointing us to Christ, who became the living Word of God. **And the Word became flesh and dwelt among us** (John 1:14). Jesus is our example; He used the Word of God himself in doing battle with Satan in the hour of His temptation.

In the book of Revelation, we are told that out of Christ's mouth will go a sharp two-edged sword in the battle of Armageddon (see Rev. 1:16; 19:21). Victory is gained with that sword. What is it? It is the Word of God, the same weapon you and I have been told we are to use as we wage spiritual warfare. I need that weapon going out of my mouth. It's powerful. Have you learned how to use it?

Paul tells us to "take" this sword and use it. It's an imperative verb, in other words, a command given with military snap and curtness. That means it is meant to be obeyed.

Discipline Required

Soldiers who complained about the weight of their armor and who laid some of it aside, were the ones who, if caught off guard, would be rendered useless if suddenly engaged in battle. All of this armor needs to be taken up and used appropriately, but there is one other offensive weapon we are told to use.

Praying Always

The second weapon of offense is prayer:

> **And pray in the Spirit on all occasions with all kinds of prayers and requests. With this in mind, be alert and always keep on praying for all the saints.**
> **Ephesians 6:18 NIV**

Good soldiers are watchful and alert at all times. Just so, the spiritual man, engaged in warfare with the enemy, through prayer keeps in touch with the Holy Spirit, laying hold of spiritual resources. All effective praying is done in the Spirit.

We must pray, and pray as we have never before prayed. Divine intervention is needed for the difficult days that lie ahead. These are days when the enemy is hard at work. Only a militant church — people equipped to do spiritual warfare — will survive the devil's attacks. God will respond to the soldier who means business for Him.

Paul, held captive in a Roman prison and waiting to die for the cause of Christ, gave a final charge to young Timothy (2 Tim. 4:1,2,5), which can be summarized as follows:
- Preach the Word.
- Be diligent at all times.

- Reprove, rebuke, and exhort whenever needed.
- Remain alert at all times.
- Bear up under persecutions.
- Evangelize your field.
- Utilize your ministry to the fullest.

The apostle wrote words of warning to the younger man that seem very applicable to us today. Paul wrote that in the last days men would not tolerate sound doctrine but would be controlled by their lusts, and in their restlessness, would seek out many false teachers and refuse the truth. (2 Tim. 4:3,4.)

A man's final words are always worth noting. I want to be able to say this at life's end. Here is what Paul said:

> **For I am already being poured out as a drink offering, and the time of my departure is at hand.**
>
> **I have fought the good fight, I have finished the race, I have kept the faith.**
>
> 2 Timothy 4:6-7

2

The Character of a
Soldier of Christ

In writing to his young disciple, Timothy, Paul explained the character of a soldier of Christ. Chapter 2 of Second Timothy says a soldier of Christ is to be:

- Strong (vv. 1,2)
- Single-minded (vv. 3,4)
- Strict (vv. 5-10)
- Secure (vv. 11-13)
- Sound of faith (vv. 14-19)
- Sanctified (vv. 20-23)
- A servant (vv. 24-26)

In other words, the consistency of God's character shines through the demeanor of the militant man who remains faithful.

But know this, that in the last days perilous times will come, Paul cautioned in Second Timothy 3:1. The perils of apostasy are very real today. Satan is out to turn this world into his own personal graveyard, but we have been promised protection from apostasy when we carefully follow the Biblical pattern and continue in the truth. (2 Tim. 3:10-17.)

Paul adds to these words to Timothy a final request for him to come to see him quickly and to bring his cloak and books, especially the parchments — copies of what we know as the Old Testament books. (2 Tim. 4:13.) In the approaching time of his near death, this warrior for the Lord requested the Scripture. Would that be your dying request?

Paul's final words rang with assurance: **To Him be glory forever and ever. Amen!** (2 Tim. 4:18). This is war — but we do not go empty-handed into battle, for God has provided weapons.

The Christian life is not a playground; it is a battlefield. Battles are won and battles are lost on battlefields. Paul cautioned, **No one engaged in warfare entangles himself with the affairs of this life, that he may please him who enlisted him as a soldier** (2 Tim. 2:4). There are some "Christians" who are so entangled in worldliness that they are Christian in name only. They do not perceive that they are losing the battle; in fact, they don't even realize that life here is being lived out on a battlefield.

The Weapons of Our Warfare

Paul told the Corinthian Christians that though we walk in the flesh, we do not war after the flesh (2 Cor. 10:3 KJV). The word *flesh* here has as its meaning "weakness." "For though we walk in weakness, in natures that are born corrupt," Paul is saying, "we do not war in our weakly fleshly nature."

The apostle had a grand perspective of a heaven to be gained, and a hell to shun. He was telling those to whom he wrote these words — and the message is for us — that we are in spiritual warfare so it requires spiritual weapons. He adds a parenthetical statement: **For the weapons of our warfare are not carnal but** mighty in God for pulling down strongholds, casting down arguments and every high thing that exalts itself against the knowledge of God, bringing every thought into captivity to the obedience of Christ (2 Cor. 10:4,5).

A Spiritual Enemy To Be Defeated

Paul says our weapons are mighty. Mighty and effective.

Let us get it into our heads our first powerful weapon is the Word of God. To use a weapon, a militant man must have confidence in it.

When Paul came to Corinth, he knew he was coming to a city corrupted by philosophy and "religion." He drew his trusty sword and depended upon the naked sharp blade of the Word to fight for him.

He could confidently declare, **For I am not ashamed of the gospel of Christ, for it is the power of God to salvation for everyone who believes....For in it the righteousness of God is revealed...** (Rom. 1:16,17).

That's the kind of confidence the Christian militant man and woman needs. This confidence in the Word is one of our weapons.

The second weapon is the presence of the Holy Spirit. Recognition of his own weakness and his humanness prompted the Apostle Paul to say that it was the power of God that overtook his flesh enabling him to wage successful warfare.

The third mighty weapon is prayer. **Now thanks be to God who always leads us in triumph in Christ,** and through us diffuses the fragrance of His knowledge in every place (2 Cor. 2:14).

We are to leave behind the sweet aroma of Christ. We aren't to "peddle the word of God," Paul says (v. 17), but in sincerity we are to speak boldly for Christ. The winsomeness of our witness, as we pray in the Spirit, asking God to put the right words in our mouth, will lead us in triumph through Christ.

3

End-Time Warfare and Catastrophic Calamities

In November 1987, while in Israel, the Lord spoke to my heart and told me it was getting late on the prophetic calendar, and that we were to be ready to help take care of suffering people. God even gave me a name — The End-Time Joseph Program to Feed the Hungry — allowing me to see and understand that we, like the Biblical Joseph, would be used to alleviate the pain that accompanies hunger. The hunger that will come upon the earth will be the result of famine, disturbances in the earth, and man's inhumanity to man.

So we have been gearing up. We have already fed and relieved the suffering of hurting humanity in many places throughout the earth, and we will continue to do so as needs come to our attention. This is being militant. And we are calling for God's people worldwide to join us in fighting hunger. I see hunger as nothing less than a tool of the devil to destroy God's people.

One of the things the Lord told me in Jerusalem is that end-time events as depicted in Matthew 24 are being accelerated now. Facts concerning the condition of the earth and its weather patterns, for instance, lead me to believe that it is later than many think. This planet is an agitated place. Great and awesome events in nature have been with us since the dawn of time, many of them catastrophic and violent, striking without warning, leaving havoc and destruction in their wake. But there does seem to be an acceleration of such events now. Notice the following:

- The decade of the '80s saw the hottest summer temperatures in this century.

- There have been more earthquakes in the world during this century than have been recorded during any century heretofore. The October 1989 earthquake in the San Francisco area had been predicted for a long time, but even with all its damage, experts were saying it was not "the big one" that is expected. About thirty-five earthquakes of a magnitude capable of being registered on the Richter Scale are recorded over the earth every day. The 1988 earthquake in Armenia had one of the largest tolls in human life in recent times with upwards to 25,000 people killed.

- There have been more natural catastrophes — floods, tornadoes, typhoons — than have ever been known before.

- There are increasing accounts of pests and pestilence with accompanying disease and suffering.

- During 1989 we began to hear more and more about a "greenhouse effect," caused by the layer of ozone around the earth being destroyed by chemical pollutants. If this really is what is happening, the world in a very few years will be very different than anything the human race has ever experienced.

These are some of the things that indicate approaching drought and famine, as well as upheavals in society and in the economy as a result.

The Lord said to me in Jerusalem that there is going to be famine as He predicted, such as the world has never known. And He said He did not want His children to die of hunger before He comes.

Some of the possible end results of trends that are being clearly seen in the climate and weather patterns include these:

> Heat waves and droughts could become commonplace, increasing the chances of crop failures, increased air pollution, severe forest fires, and human suffering...as the sea level rises, flooding could spill into costal living areas, beaches, wetlands, and estuaries (which) could become inundated by rising ocean waters....

Because of increased temperatures and more frequent drought, regions such as the American grain belt could become much drier and warmer during the critical growing season. Climates suitable for farming could shift, sometimes to regions of the world where soils are not suitable for agriculture. Water shortages would make irrigation difficult and expensive. Deserts and grasslands would be expected to spread as forests shrink.[1]

Preparation Years

Whatever the reasons for the coming famine, the Lord has given us warning and time to prepare, just at He always has told His "prophets" what lies ahead (Amos 3:7) and as He always has warned His people.

In the midst of the increasing catastrophes — earthquakes, forest fires, hurricanes, tornadoes — we can see God's hand mitigating the consequences. His grace is protecting us from the worst. Most of these catastrophes have destroyed property and resources, but there have been comparatively few deaths, considering the severity of some of these events.

Just as the prophet Amos warned the nation of Israel in his day, God is using these occurrences to warn His people of worse things to come. Amos was told:

> I also withheld rain from you,
> When there were still three months to the harvest.
> I made it rain on one city,
> I withheld rain from another city.
> One part was rained upon,
> And where it did not rain the part withered.
>
> Amos 4:7

Weather experts say that the Mount St. Helens volcanic eruption would have caused devastatingly cold weather across the world, bringing food surpluses dangerously low, except for one thing: a "lucky accident."[2]

> Nineteen eighty-one missed having a summer like 1816 [ice and snow in the summer and almost no harvest worldwide] for one main reason. Unusually, the blast from Mount St. Helens [in 1980] was directed sideways, not upward.

Historians call 1816, the year after the volcanic eruption of Mount Tembora, "the year without a summer." Do you really believe a "lucky accident" caused that blast in 1981 to go sideways instead of upward into the stratosphere where the dust would have affected weather worldwide? God was giving us time to see what is coming. Now, He has given me a mandate to actively prepare for those times of famine that lie ahead.

The Lord told me there were ten thousand pastors who would become a part of this effort to feed the hungry, and it has been so exciting everywhere I have gone since then. The Lord is raising up an army of militant Christians!

On a trip to Peru, there were forty young people who joined us. In Russia, there were seventeen. We do not ask them to go. We just give them the location and the date, and they show up. Some of them get there before I do, and some after, but they come, and they pray and lay hands on people.

In Peru one night, we had so many people finding God, the crowd was thirty feet deep, clear across the auditorium, which was a former theater. I turned that bunch of preachers loose, and it was a glorious sight as these pastors began to pray the Peruvians through to victory. It was a beautiful, beautiful sight.

Adopting Winning Strategies

The Church is going to win on every front. The devil cannot do a thing about it. We are going to take territory away from him. But in order to do that, we must move into offensive warfare.

A lot of preachers do not want to believe me about The End-Time Joseph Program to Feed the Hungry, but one day, they will say, "Why didn't we help him?"

This program is one way of using offensive warfare.

You can only fight from two basic strategies: defensive and offensive. Generals who win wars are those who fight offensively, those who take the initiative.

Someone asked Napoleon once why he won all those battles, and he said, "Because I'm there just a few minutes before they expect me."

He was an offensive warrior and a fighter. The End-Time Joseph Program, named after one of Jacob's sons, Joseph, who saved all of Egypt in a time of famine, is an offensive strategy. It means getting prepared so that the enemy's best weapons have no effect on you.

[1]"Global Warming: The Heat Is On," *Conversation '89, National Wildlife Federation's Environmental Digest*, Vol. 7, No. 7, July 30, 1989, pp. 8,9.

[2]Gribbin, John. *Future Weather and the Greenhouse Effect* (New York: Delacorte Press/Eleanor Friede. Copyright 1982 by John and Mary Gribbin), p. 157.

4

The Future of the Militant Church

It is time for the Church to be offensive in battle against the devil.

In Matthew 16:18, we see Jesus in conversation with Peter. **And I also say to you that you are Peter, and on this rock I will build My church, and the gates of Hades shall not prevail against it.**

The name *Peter* (Greek, *Petros*), means rock or rockman. In the next phrase Christ used *petra* ("upon this rock"), a feminine form for "rock," not a name. Christ used a play on words. He does not say "upon you, Peter" or "upon your successors," but "on this rock" — upon this divine revelation and profession of faith in Christ. "I will build" shows that the formation of the church was still in the future. It began on the day of Pentecost (Acts 2). The word "church" appears in the gospels only here and in Matthew 18:17.

Who is "the Rock"? The Rock is Christ. The true church is built upon Christ: **For no other foundation can anyone lay than that which is laid, which is Jesus Christ** (1 Cor. 3:11).

It's interesting to note that the Church was still future when Jesus spoke these words to Peter. The Church actually came into existence after the death, resurrection, and ascension of Christ, and the sending of the Holy Spirit. When Christ said, "I will build My church," this was future.

"The Gates of Hell"

I have heard military men speak of war as "hell." When the spiritually militant Church gets moving for the Lord Jesus Christ, they will know they are in a battle as real as the kind of living hell servicemen speak of. The devil will pit all his forces against the Church that is fighting sin.

But we know the end of the story. We've read the Book! Jesus promised that **the gates of hell shall not prevail against it** [the church] (Matt. 16:18).

The Church wins!

The Future of the Church

The future of the Church is very important. The devil hates the Church. The Church is hated by secularists — the educational systems, the various forms of media, and the different groups and organizations that are humanist oriented.

America's young people today have grown up not being taught to respect the Church. Many of them have never been inside a church. But I believe that now is the time for us to strike aggressively against the devil, against sin, against every enemy of righteousness, against everything that is against God. This means reaching out to young people with strong church programs and events that will attract them. A church that does not have a vision to reach and hold onto its youth is not being militant.

It is amazing to me that people still are afraid of communism when it is crumbling before our very eyes. In seventy years, communism has run its course.

In Estonia we rented the city auditorium, a gorgeous, beautiful building. The KGB in Moscow called the person who had rented us the building.

They said, "We hear an evangelist and his group who were here in Leningrad have arrived there."

And this woman who was in charge said, "Yes, they're here."

"We hear you have rented them the city auditorium."

"Yes," she said, "that's right."

"Why did you do that?" the caller asked.

"None of your business," she said, and hung up on him! A few years ago, you would have had your head cut off for that. But she just laughed and said, "I've just told them in Moscow it is none of their business what I do over here. I am running this thing."

We had so many people attending that meeting that hundreds were turned away. Russia may think that her strategy of freedom is buying time, but actually, the state of the economy and the lack of well-being in communist countries proves communism has failed.

The Church needs to be ready to fill the vacuum. We cannot do it on defensive operations, however. Whether it is your church, your business, or even your home, you cannot win with a defensive strategy of spiritual warfare.

Become Aggressive Before God

The Church is going to have to be aggressive before God and teach her families what God wants them to be, because the Church is people. Church people are going to have to stand and fight the devil every inch of the way. He cannot take over the Church or your home unless you let him.

We have too many "rocking chair Christians." If you are going to sit in a rocking chair, you do not need any armor. All you need is a pillow at your back, so you can take a little snooze. Too many Christians are saying, "Pray me out of my troubles. Pray me out of my troubles!"

Those who come down to the altar to be prayed for much of the time are defensive people. It is about time everyone of us becomes a soldier and puts on the whole armor of God that we might be able to stand in the evil day. This is the evil day.

We must be able to prevail, and we are going to do it. We have the finest group of young preachers living today that the world has ever had. We have men who are afraid of nothing, young men who are leading their churches, teaching them how to prevail.

Get off the defensive, and get offensive! It is time to go after the devil and go after sin. The devil has quickened his efforts to defeat the Church. He is bringing every kind of corruption into our homes, schools and communities, even into our churches. It is time to fight him back. It is time we determine where his next strike will be and get there ahead of him, instead of playing "catch-up" all the time.

We need to begin to ask, "What can we do to overthrow the devil?"

In the rest of this book, I want to show you how you can renew your mind from passive acceptance of defeat to a militant moving forth in victory.

When a general plans a new battle, everything changes. He plots a new strategy, has new maps drawn up, counts the cost in men and material, draws orders to have men and equipment moved to new places.

In your own life, when you come to a new year, things change. You have to write new dates on your checks. Every time you write a letter, you write down a new date. You have started something new.

The correct attitude toward the coming battle, the coming year, or whatever new thing is occurring in your life is probably the most important first step in bringing victory in that situation.

So I want to talk about seven winning attitudes, or in the military analogy, seven winning positions you can take in accomplishing victory in the Lord's service for the future. I also want to give you seven losing positions that will cost you the victory.

We believe the present is very important. Many believe we are living in prophetic times. The Church needs to move victoriously into the coming days.

What will be the new move of God?

How are you going to discover the new direction of the Lord?

I believe the key is in your attitude toward God, how you think about God and how you think about the world in which you live.

5

The Stance of the Militant Christian

I have identified what I believe are to be seven winning attitudes that will equip us to defeat the enemy. In military terminology they would be termed "positions." What is to be the stance of the militant Christian, the position he takes in his daily walk?

We are to:
Think militantly
Pray militantly
Speak militantly
Give militantly
Go out militantly
Resist militantly
Love militantly
Let's look at each of these.

Thinking Militantly

Perhaps you are wondering what I mean by living offensively and aggressively. When I say God's people need to move into a more aggressive attitude and to think militantly, what am I implying?

The word aggressive has both negative and positive connotations. I am using it in the positive sense. Among its many dictionary definitions, the word *aggressive* means behavior marked by combative readiness [a fighter]; marked by driving forceful energy or initiative. It implies militancy. Militancy can mean a fighting spirit that is bold, brash, crude, pushy and officious. But in its more positive sense, militancy means aggressively active as in devotion to a cause.

Certainly Christians have every reason to be aggressively militant as we live out our devotion to the cause of Christ.

We are God's winners, not losers. We are to be **the head and not the tail** (Deut. 28:13). This happens as we are obedient to observe carefully God's commandments.

You have to start with your thinking in order to do this. I can take you through the Bible and show you how the people called "heroes and heroines of the faith" thought aggressively. We must think with great strength, **For as he** [a man] **thinks in his heart, so is he** (Prov. 23:7).

Study God's Strategy To Think Militantly

There has never been a great general who did not sit down and calculate how to defeat the enemy. A great general will consider the terrain — mountains, desert, woods, or cities and towns — the distance, and what the opposing army's strength is.

We should study how best to take nations. We should ask the Lord how to reach a nation with the Gospel.

Some years ago, the Lord told me, "If you go to the capital city of a Third-world country and build a mighty center of evangelism, you can evangelize the entire nation." So that's where I went. This was, I felt, my calling, but not everyone, obviously, has the same calling.

Back in 1950 the Lord told me, "I want you to be the first one to do this," so we went and surveyed Manila in the Philippines.

People said to us, "Oh, no. We don't believe it that way. We think you should start a school and train the nationals."

I said, "Which ones? The unsaved ones? How are you going to train something you don't have? It seems to me as if revival comes first."

At any rate, we went to Manila, and at first, it seemed the devil was beating us. We went to church a number of times with no one there but my wife, myself, and our boys.

You ask, "What did you do?"

I had church. We sang, we prayed, we shouted, and I preached. We did everything but take up an offering. There is no need to take up an offering if there is no one there but your family. But we were determined to have a church in that city.

Then a girl in jail was bitten severly on her body by devils, and suddenly the newspapers were full of the story of this strange phenomenon every day for three weeks. (The entire story is told in Chapter 14 of my book *Alien Entities*.[1])

I was so busy trying to build a church that I was not reading newspapers or listening to the radio and

I knew nothing about it. By the time it was bought to my attention, she had cursed one doctor who had laughed at her, and he had died. The head man at the prison kicked her; she cursed him, and he died. They did not get sick; they just dropped dead.

Fear was over the entire city, but I did not know anything about it, I was so busy building. I learned then that you have to get outside your own church. If you do not, you are never going to bless this world.

But I was doing something courageous. I had bought a B-52 hangar and was building a place to seat two thousand people when I only had five at that point.

Everyone said, "He's crazy, he's crazy, he's crazy!"

But I said, "What I am doing is like a farmer who builds a barn before the harvest time. If he doesn't, he will lose the harvest. I am just building the barn. God is going to bring in the harvest, and the barn is going to be full."

The day we dedicated that church, you could not get within two blocks of the place. They were jam-packed inside the building. They were there to see what God had done.

God used that poor little seventeen-year-old girl in jail to begin our ministry in the Philippines. That is strategy. We need to study God's strategy in the Word and in Christian books. If you earnestly seek Him and ask Him to show you His strategy, you will begin to see how He operates.

God's Opening Wedge

In the natural, it would seem a demon-possessed girl would have nothing to do with my church. However, the Lord brought the situation to my attention, sent me over to the prison to take deliverance to her, and that brought my church and ministry to the attention of the public and government officials.

The deliverance of Clarita Villanueva was God's weapon, His wedge in the closed door of the Philippines. Once He had His foot in the door, it was easy to push on in and take the territory.

As soon as the girl was free, I was able to get permission from the mayor to complete our building and also to preach six weeks in the city park — the first Protestant preacher to ever get anything from the government without paying a lot of money in bribes.

In the meantime, God had already moved on people in America to send us materials needed for a great revival.

Without even knowing what we were doing, Gordon Lindsay in Texas sent us thousands of magazines with testimonies in them. Also, without knowing what we were doing, Oral Roberts sent me a film on healing, complete with a projector, a screen, and everything to go with it.

Through Ruben Candelaria, superintendent of the Methodist churches in the Manila area, God miraculously opened up the churches of the city to us for services. I went to all the main churches preaching, showing the film, and distributing the magazines. By the time we went into the park meetings, the whole city was aflame.

The Taytay Methodist Church paid for me to go on the radio. They paid for 15 minutes after the evening news on a powerful station which covered the whole nation. Every night, right after the news, I talked about what was happening in Manila. People came from all over the country to attend the meetings. Not one city was unrepresented. They came to see the miracles that were taking place. Every kind of miracle imaginable was witnessed.[2]

In that one revival, we saw 150,000 people saved. That was the most remarkable thing I have ever seen. How could that come about? God initiated it, and His strategy brought it about. He defeated the strong man over that nation through me.

I had been praying, "How can we move this nation? What can we do about this nation?"

Then God exploded the whole thing.

I believe the Church can yet have an influence on America, on the states, and on the cities and towns.

We must not only think militantly, we must study God's strategy, so that we will be ready to cooperate with the Holy Spirit, ready to be obedient, when He is ready to move.

The disciples and those people of the early Church had absolutely no media available — no newspapers or magazines, no radio or television. They had no big ministries and staffs. Yet they reached the world. How much easier it should be for us today.

There are ways of reaching everyone on the face of the earth. There are men who are out doing that today. This generation is living in the greatest time in the history of the world. More is happening right now than I have ever known to happen before.

Aren't you glad you are alive? I am glad to be alive in this day and hour.

[1]Sumrall, Lester. *Alien Entities* (Tulsa: Harrison House, 1984), p. 139.

[2]Ibid, p. 139.

6

Pray Militantly

The second winning position spoken to my heart by the Lord is to pray militantly.

Mary, Queen of Scots, used to say that she feared the prayers of the fiery Protestant theologian John Knox more than all of the armies of France and England put together. John Knox knew how to pray aggressively!

Too many of us kneel down and go to sleep on our knees, or we read a few verses in the Bible, and the next thing you know, our heads are on top of the Book. You are not knocking out the enemy that way.

In the early days of American history, the generals who won were the generals who prayed militantly.

One day a farmer approaching the camp (at Valley Forge) heard an earnest voice. On coming nearer, he saw George Washington on his knees, his cheeks wet with tears, praying to God.

He returned home and said to his wife: "George Washington will succeed! The Americans will win their independence!"

"What makes you think so, Isaac?" asked his wife.

The farmer replied: "I heard him pray,
Hannah, out in the woods today, and the Lord
will surely hear his prayer. He will, Hannah;
thee may rest assured He will."[1]

Why was that farmer so sure God would hear
General George Washington? Because, I am sure, he
was praying militantly. Great things depended on his
prayer, and great things depend on our prayers.

Before the Battle of Gettysburg, when the fate of
the nation was hanging in the balance, President
Abraham Lincoln was calm and assured. His generals
wanted to know why and this is what he answered.

"I spent last night in prayer before the
Lord. He has given me the assurance that our
cause will triumph and that the nation will be
preserved."[2]

In our time, General Eisenhower once said:

"Prayer gives you the courage to make the
decisions you must make in crisis and then
the confidence to leave the result to a Higher
Power."[3]

Prayer is not for the purpose of changing God's
mind. He already wants us to win and to be victorious,
overcoming children more than we want to. Prayer is
for changing situations, circumstances, and people's
hearts. Prayer is for overcoming and defeating the
demons of hell assigned to hinder Christians.

The World's Greatest Untapped Resource

I believe prayer to be the world's greatest untapped
resource. Prayer is not something you merely think or

talk about. Prayer is something you do — God's power made available to mankind, a great resource. Yet, for the most part, prayer is not properly understood.

Why is that so? Because there is a mystique, a secret, that seems to have placed effective prayer beyond the reach of most believers.

But the power resources of prayer are attainable. Prayer is a force to be used, a tool to be utilized, a mighty weapon to be deployed. This becomes clear and plain as we read: **Finally, my brethren, be strong in the Lord** [or, in Jehovah] **and in the power of His might. Put on the whole armor of God** [that's what prayer will teach you to do], **that you may be able to stand against the wiles of the devil** (Eph. 6:10,11).

One little known fact God desires to make plain is that it is possible to stand against the tricks of the devil, but to do so, you must certainly learn the secrets of prayer.

For the weapons of our warfare are not carnal but mighty in God for pulling down strongholds (2 Cor. 10:4). Our weapons are not physical or mental; they are spiritual. One of the best of our weapons is prayer.

Prayer Power in Action

On more than one occasion Jesus' disciples witnessed a demonstration of prayer power. **And when they** (the disciples) **had prayed, the place where they were assembled together was shaken; and they were all filled with the Holy Spirit, and they spoke the word of God with boldness** (Acts 4:31).

Here are the conditions: the believers assembled together and prayed. Here are the results: The place was shaken; they were filled with the power of the Holy Spirit; then they spoke the Word of God — not with backwardness nor fear — with great boldness. First they prayed, then the power came.

If we can get the churches in our land to reach out to God through prayer, we will discover resources of strength, blessing, anointing, goodness, and mercies we never dreamed about. If we can convince the world that it is prayer time in our land, the result will be an anointing of power previously unknown.

There are battles that can be won only when we pray. Victories — even over demonic forces — can be ours through prayer.

Let's Get Our People To Pray

Prayer, when used as it was designed and intended, is a tremendous force, a terrible weapon against the enemy. I am talking of prayer that can exert a world-changing influence. When it is truly understood and faithfully used, prayer is the greatest source of untapped energy the world has ever known.

To bring about such prayer requires a change in our thinking and in our praying habits. Such prayer among the people of God can change the Church of Jesus Christ in America and all around the world. It matters not if you are reading this book in the United States, or in the Philippines, or in Japan, or in South America. Whoever you are, wherever you live, I am assuring you that by your prayers, you can receive and set into motion the power of God. Only through prayer is this possible.

United Prayer Produces United Results

Cornelius learned this when he prayed. Cornelius was **a devout man and one who feared God with all his household** (Acts 10:2). Praying together as a family multiplies your prayer power. God tells us that one can chase a thousand, and two can put ten thousand to flight. (see Deut. 32:30.) As Cornelius learned, when you unite your home in prayer, you become like an army ready for battle. Prayer can change a person, but it can also change entire families!

When Cornelius and his family prayed unitedly, God performed miracles. He sent for Peter, who was one hundred miles away in the city of Joppa. Peter came and preached to Cornelius, resulting in that man's entire family receiving the infilling of the Holy Spirit.

None of these things happened haphazardly. They came about through prayer.

Just as prayer changed Cornelius' life and the lives of his family, prayer can change your life and the lives of those around you. By learning the secrets of prayer, as Cornelius did, you could also be remembered as a person who changed this world and the world to come. Prayer is that powerful!

Prayer Releases Dynamic Energy

You can help others by your prayers. The Apostle Paul spoke of this dimension of prayer: **You also helping together in prayer for us, that thanks may be**

given by many persons on our behalf for the gift granted to us through many (2 Cor. 1:11).

You see, you can become a prayer partner; you can join with others and become a means of "helping together in prayer." Cornelius helped his family through prayer. You can do the same. You can bless others; you can help missionaries; you can help your pastor and the community and government. All of this and much, much more can be accomplished through your unselfish praying.

You can literally release prisoners by praying. When Herod imprisoned Peter, **constant prayer was offered to God for him by the church** (Acts 12:5). God responded by sending an angel to release Peter. That's the kind of power that's still available to God's people through their prayers! That's the same power that you and your prayer group can have.

Pray militantly, aggressively. Say, "God, I come against communism [or pornography, or abortion, or whatever it is]. Confuse wicked world leaders to where they do not know what to do, do not even know what month to plant grain, do not know how to handle the cleanup from an earthquake. Just let them be confused. Let them know there is a God in heaven and that they do not have Him."

Pray against the evil in our land. Many abortion clinics in Ohio went bankrupt because of a young minister's militancy against them. So much damage was done that they sued him for $11.5 million dollars. Then they saw that Rod Parsley was happy about the suit as he went around gathering lawyers to fight them.

So they said, "Well, just forget it. We have decided not to sue you."

His church prayed militantly. When they went out on the street corners, they prayed with strength and vigor and power and will. They went out in the whole armor of God.

Prayer is one of our main weapons in these spiritual battles, but unless we pray militantly, our prayers are not effective. Prayer also allows us to learn God's strategy in every situation. Get alone with the Lord, and pray militantly. You will receive inspiration and creative ideas from the Holy Spirit which will bring victory.

Too Many Wrong Prayers

We have too many soft prayers, too many apologetic prayers. The breadth, the extent, of our praying is as large as our asking. God expects us to reach out to the farthest horizons we can imagine, and to use all the strength and all the power that He has made available to us — all of it in Jesus' name.

So you can see, prayer is not just the mere recitation of words. Prayer is a relationship — with God and with Jesus, His Son. Prayer is the speaking of loving words, a love lyric to our Lord and Savior Jesus Christ.

Prayer is a personal connection with God. Prayer is alive. Prayer is inspiring. Prayer is powerful, energizing, dynamic! Prayer revitalizes the one who prays. But prayer is not just spiritual recreation. Prayer is doing battle with the invisible forces of darkness.

When we went to the Philippines, we went prepared for a big church. We took an electric organ, a piano, and other things. We had tons and tons of freight. I am the only missionary in history, I believe, who took his offering bags with him.

I had just been to see Oral Roberts, and he had those pretty purple bags, which were new at that time. I bought twelve of them, put them in my suitcase, and took them to the mission field.

You say, "What did you do with them?"

After the church's dedication day, I filled them up in Jesus' name every time we had church. That was being a little aggressive too, I suppose.

But then we went to the West Coast to get a boat to the Philippines, we found there was a strike on the docks, and no boats would go. But into the harbor came a Dutch freighter that was going to Manila, so we took passage on it.

We found another missionary family that already had taken passage on that boat to Manila. They were Methodists. The father was a handsome, tall gentleman, and he and his wife had five or six children. My wife and I had two boys then.

So I said, "Let's have worship together every morning," and he agreed.

Then I said, "As you are the older, you lead the worship the first morning."

After the stewards cleaned up the little area where we ate in the dining room, both families gathered around a table, and this missionary brought in a stack of books. He was burdened down with them.

He would read a few lines from one, then say, "And Dr. so-and-so said this," and he would read from another liberal preacher-author. He did not have a Bible with him, but he quoted six or eight of his books, then he closed them and prayed.

He said, "Our father, we are so sinful. We sin every day. Forgive us of our many sins," and so forth.

When he got through, I felt so badly, I had to go out and get some fresh air. It was awful!

But I thought, "I'm going to help you tomorrow morning. That's my time."

The next morning, I only had one book — the Bible. I opened it up, and I read, then I prayed, "Glory be to God! How wonderful it is to be saved and to be a missionary to the Philippines."

I thought, "That helped him" — until the next morning, when it was his time again. He must have brought in twenty books this time. He came in and put them all on the table.

Again, it was "Dr. so-and-so said this, and Dr. something-else said that," and he gave us little tidbits from these theologians.

Then he closed his books and prayed, "Our Father, we're so sinful. Every day we sin. We are so sorry for our sins."

It was just like the prayer he had prayed two mornings before. He had not gotten anything out of my example. Again, it was so sad that I had to go out on the deck for some fresh air, and again, I said, "I'll try again tomorrow."

I worked all day on what to read and how to pray to lift him up, and the next morning I read the Word. His little children learned to love me very much. They liked hearing the Word. I read to them from the Bible and prayed an exuberant prayer of glory, victory, and power.

And I said, "For sure that prayer helped him."

But the next morning, here he came with more books. It seemed as if he had worked all day and night researching. He sat down and said, "It's my time." Then he read from the books, a little here and a little there.

Then he said, "My Father, we're so sinful. We sin every day. . . ." I was really upset.

When he had finished praying, I asked him to talk with me. I said, "Now, there are only two women on board. They are your wife and my wife. What is all this sinning business you're doing every day — Would you tell me more about it?"

"Oh," he said, "I'm not doing anything wrong or sinful."

"Well, you said you did. You said you had sinned all day long. I don't see what else there is on this ship to be sinning about." I could see the wheels going around in his head.

He said, "Well, that's the way I was taught to pray."

I asked, "Have you not heard me praying the past three mornings?"

"But I have never heard anyone pray like that before," he objected.

"Well please listen to me," I said, "we've got thirty days together on this boat."

That man became marvelously changed by the time we got to the Philippines.

He said, "I'm not going to teach in a theological school, and I'm not going to pastor a church. I am going to raise up churches!"

For a good while, he would call me about once a month and say, "Sumrall, I just held a meeting over here, built them a church, and now they have a pastor in it."

I would say, "Great! Now go do it again."

Next month, here would come another call, and he would say, "I have been over here four weeks, had a mighty revival, and many got saved. We have started a church and put a pastor in it."

He was raising up more churches than all the other ministers of his denomination in the nation put together.

How did he do that?

He got aggressive. He got mad at the devil. He stopped making apologies to God. If you are consistently going to apologize to God, you will have weak prayers that will never win victories. God wants you to pray with force.

It Is Time To Get Aggressive

You do not have to pray kneeling down. You can dance as you pray. You can swing your arms when you pray. That will keep you awake. But above all, you must pray against the devil. Pray against sin. Pray against wickedness in high places. We are going to have to initiate aggressive praying — powerful praying.

Jesus prayed with mighty strength.

Elijah prayed with strength.

> Elijah was a man with a nature like ours, and he prayed earnestly [militantly] that it would not rain; and it did not rain on the land for three years and six months.
>
> And he prayed again, and the heaven gave rain, and the earth produced its fruit.
>
> James 5:17,18

Elijah was one little preacher with a nature like ours, the Apostle James said, but he beat seven hundred and fifty false prophets. He called fire down from heaven, and that is no pipsqueak prayer. He was in a life-and-death situation. Without victory, he was a dead man. But it was not Elijah who died, but four hundred and fifty false prophets, and Elijah did the swordwork himself. (1 Kings 18:19.)

Elijah wound himself up militantly and said, "Rain: Don't come to this part of the world for the next three-and-one-half years, and I'm in charge!"

How would you like to be able to do that? It did not rain for the period of time Elijah had prayed. I will bet you could hear him for a mile. He was not a little, sweet, tender thing that you could not hear above a whisper.

People who say, "I can't pray out loud," will yell at their kids at the top of their voices almost breaking their eardrums! Why can't they pray out loud? The devil is hindering them. He does not want them to pray loudly, so he drops thoughts of fear or pride into their minds.

God wants His children to know that it is time to get aggressive for him. You must get aggressive in your prayer life to have victory everywhere else. When you start meaning your prayers, God will answer them.

I prayed, "Lord, how can we be a people away from the defensive and on the offensive forever?"

I hate being defensive, trying to protect myself. I hate that. I would far rather take the initiative all the time, especially against the devil. Keep him on the run all the time. Beat him down. You can be God's champion warrior if you want to be.

This is the time to say:

> In the name of the Lord, my attitude toward prayer is that I am going to pray militantly — as Moses did, as Elijah did, and as Jesus did. Let my prayers be powerful, prayers that change things. God help me to pray aggressively.

That is a good winning position to take, is it not? Change your prayer style, and you can pray militantly before the Lord.

Prayer Is Invincible

Prayer is invincible. It cannot be subdued. Nobody can hinder or prevent the operation of prayer power. Rulers of great nations have had their laws and decrees defied and altered by prayer.

The evil leaders of Babylonia influenced King Darius to defy the power of prayer by casting Daniel into the lions' den. (see Dan. 6:10-23.) Daniel was unscathed — living proof of the invincible power of prayer.

Wicked Haman learned — too late — the invincible power of prayer. His clever manipulations served only to hang him upon his own gallows and the one he built for his enemy. (See Esth. 7:10.)

It has always been so.

Prayer can destroy enemy powers and evil forces. Prayer can build the Kingdom of God. This has always been God's intent.

Prayer operates in the lives of those who have provided God with clean, righteous vessels, in which His Holy Spirit dwells, in which egotism and self-sufficiency have been eradicated. It is in such lives — in which material things have faded and the spiritual life is in proper focus — that God chooses to display His unlimited power.

Evil, self-aggrandizing forces rule the world we live in — political and economic forces, power-hungry forces that are humanly irresistible, immovable, indomitable, insurmountable, impregnable, unconquerable, and unyielding. Yet all these forces are but "paper tigers" in the face of anointed prayer.

Before World War II, France believed its Maginot Line invincible. Germany proved it wrong by simply going around the ends. Germany believed its blitzkrieg manner of warfare was invincible. Yet it was to learn that its "best" would succumb to a superior force.

Our enemy believes himself to be invincible.

Yet when you and I discover the secrets of and appropriate the inestimably superior powers of prayer — the truly invincible **whole armor of God** (Eph. 6:13), the defensive and offensive glories of prayer — we will move into prayer against the enemies of God, the enemies of righteousness, with an assurance, with a joyous abandon, and with an effectiveness we have never known.

When faced with such divine power, all earthly powers are subject to defeat. All earthly powers, whether political, economic, or military, are subject to the power of prayer.

Prayer has no equal. The power of prayer does not change. It stands when all other powers fail. World systems change; ideologies change; balances of world power change; balances of economics change. But the power of prayer that is available to us, the power that streams from the Almighty, the Maker of heaven and earth, will never fail. It cannot be defeated.

My friend, the secrets of prayer can be yours. And when you discover them, they will fill you with living energy. You will indeed be able to **mount up with wings like eagles, ...and not faint** (Is. 40:31).

[1]Tan, Paul Lee. Encyclopedia of 7700 Illustrations (Rockville: Assurance Publishers, 1979), *Prayer: Washington Will Succeed,* #4529, p. 1037.

[2]Ibid, *Prayer: Lincoln's Serenity,* #4609, pp. 1056, 1057.

[3]Ibid, *Prayer: Epigram,* #4567, p. 1045.

7
Develop a Militant Voice

A militant voice speaks and sings aggressively. There has never been a victorious army that did not have a song. When an army wins, the soldiers sing as loudly as they can. Only soldiers going home in defeat have no song.

Some churches and some kinds of Christians have been criticized because of their energetic singing. However, if anything, we are just getting tuned up! In other words, you have not seen anything yet. And you can tell the devil we said so!

I like aggressive singing. We do not have to wait until the sermon starts in order to come against the devil, come against him in the songs. Tell him what champions we are. Sing of the glory of God. Sing of His majesty. Sing of the victories that are flowing in our hearts. Hallelujah!

Thank God for a new song. We will sing new songs that bring joy. God wants us to sing with mighty aggressiveness, with power, with authority in Jesus' name. I like militant singing.

The Word directs us to sing a new song, and I believe those new songs are to be sung militantly:

Sing to Him a new song;
Play skillfully with a shout of joy.

For the word of the Lord is right,
And all His work is done in truth.

Psalm 33:3,4

Oh, sing to the Lord a new song!
    Sing to the Lord, all the earth.
Sing to the Lord, bless His name;
    Proclaim the good news of His
salvation from day to day.

Psalm 96:1,2

Oh, sing to the Lord a new song!
    For He has done marvelous things;
His right hand and His holy arm have
    gained Him the victory.

Psalm 98:1

Praise the Lord!

Sing to the Lord a new song,
And His praise in the congregation of saints.

Psalm 149:1

All of those admonitions came from psalmists and King David; however, singing a new song is also talked about in the very last book of the Bible.

And they sang a new song, saying:

"You are worthy to take the scroll,
And to open its seals;
For You were slain,
And have redeemed us to God
by Your blood
Out of every tribe and tongue and people and nation,
And have made us kings and priests to our God;
And we shall reign on the earth."

Revelation 5:9,10

So we see that even in heaven, there will be the singing of new songs. I do not believe those new songs were sung meekly or in a weak voice in David's day nor will they be sung that way in heaven. No! Singing in Bible days was militant (Neh. 12:27-43):

• The tribe of Judah went out first in battle, praising the Lord and singing.

• The singers sang loudly when Nehemiah dedicated the wall of Jerusalem so that the joy of Jerusalem was heard afar off.

Militant singing pleases the angels; the devil does not enjoy it. I think I would rather please the angels and please the Holy Spirit. We need to let the devil know that we mean what we sing. Let there be the ring of a king in our hearts when we sing. He is alive! He is alive!

God wants the congregation to sing militantly as well as the leaders. It is easy to come into church and be so comfortable that when you walk out, all you want is a good dinner.

If someone says, "How was the service?" and there has been no militancy present, you can say, "Oh, it was nice. It was good." But your mind is on lunch or dinner. If you sing militantly, you will get more out of the service and forget your stomach.

We are in warfare. We are going to be in some heavy battles. The Church is tired of being pushed around by the devil.

More Christians should begin to compose new choruses, to ask God for those new songs. Give the songs the Lord inspires to the song leader, the worship leader, or the pastor.

Say, "Come on, let's get with it. This is the way I feel about God."

Get the people moving stronger and more militantly.

Speak Militantly

Not only should we sing militantly, but we should be speaking militantly. That will make enemies, I must warn you in advance. Speak clearly and forcefully, and other people may say, "You want to fight, don't you?"

You must say, "Yes, I do. I want to fight the devil. I want to fight evil. I want to fight wrongdoing."

I do not think the Church today has a militant speech pattern. I do not believe that when many of us speak, people can tell which side we are on.

The Bible says that Jesus did not speak as the Pharisees, but that He spoke with authority, as a commander has to speak. (See Mark 1:22 and Luke 4:36.)

Pharisees prided themselves on their "reasoned" speech, meaning, "Perhaps the scripture means this, and perhaps it means that." And they took great pride in being able to "comment" on the law and the prophets and "interpret" the books of the Old Testament. They debated endlessly.

But they never authoritatively spoke out the Word in a spiritual sense. On the other hand, they were very rigid in holding to the works or the actions that came out of their interpretations, whitewashing the outside while not observing the laws according to the Spirit.

There was something about the voice of Jesus that was different from that of everyone else. God wants us to speak with the authority that comes from knowing the Word.

Some Christians ought to get in front of a mirror, look at, and listen to themselves to see what other people are seeing when they are talking.

God wants people today who will talk out of their spirits, talk out of their total beings. Wherever you are, learn to speak with divine strength. Let the world know that you are one of the mighty children of God.

There are people today who would say, "You want to be careful of Brother Sumrall. He uses strong language."

I say, "Yes, that's right! I use the same kind of language the Apostle Paul used."

I look through the dictionary for strong words. I have taken the world "can't" out of my vocabulary.

I say, **I can do all things through Christ who strengthens me** (Phil. 4:13).

Be a "God Pleaser"

Learn to speak with power, with vigor.

Every actor who ever lived practiced. Every trial lawyer practices — even to the movements he makes — because no matter how much truth he has on his side, unless he makes his arguments strongly, the jurors or the judge will not believe him. If he does not speak with power, his words fall to the floor and die.

So it is with Christians. We must speak the truth with authority. This is a time for speaking strong. This is a time to let the world know what we believe about certain things.

There is only one attitude you need to get into, and that is what the Lord told me years ago: Other people's heads are not the place for my happiness. In other words, people's opinions of me are not what should be influencing my actions and my life.

If you go around trying to please people — dear me, the problems you will have! You can please this one and displease that one. Then you go over to please that one and displease another one. Leave them all alone, and please God. Say what He wants you to say. Be what He wants you to be.

If you are going to be a "man-pleaser," you will never be a "God-pleaser."

This is the time to speak frankly and aggressively against sin. We have developed into a society today in which sin is not sin. "Sin" is "my problem," "my way of life," "my choice," and on and on with terms that cover up right and wrong.

Homosexuality is not considered sin, although AIDS is a dreadful consequence. The world will spend billions of dollars to find a cure for AIDS but refuse to tell men to leave men alone and find wives.

We live in a weird world today. Instead of teaching young men and women to live morally upright lives and be committed to one husband or wife, high schools pass out condoms. Then billions more dollars go into dealing with the results of promiscuity and broken homes, and abused wives and children. Millions of babies are killed before birth, but the entire world gets sentimental over three whales caught in the ice.

If you are afraid to speak for fear of hurting someone's feelings, then you are not going to speak militantly. There is only one person whose feelings I am afraid to hurt, and that is Jesus.

Of course, I am talking about speaking out strongly for the things of the Lord. I am not talking about being aggressive concerning your own whims or talking strongly against a member of your family or church. I am only talking about being strong in what you say for Jesus and for the Kingdom of God.

Some of you can be very strong on football and very weak on salvation. You must get your strength in the right place. What the Lord wants us to have in this time is an attitude of speaking militantly.

Jesus wants us to know that we have finally gotten into an army, that we have finally put on the whole armor of God, and that, finally, the Church is going to speak as Jesus spoke, so the world will know where we stand.

The world does not know where many Christians stand today. But I want them to know where I stand.

The Israelites who marched around the walls of Jericho on that seventh day certainly did not speak in a soft voice. If they had, the battle would have been lost. And if we speak softly today, we are going to lose some battles.

When we began to build our church in South Bend, Indiana, seventy-two local people signed a petition against us. We did not know there were that many people who lived within two miles of us! They came out of the woodwork. They were at a hearing for our building permit.

They were saying, "There are such beautiful trees there, and we don't want this man taking down the trees."

It was our church property, and they did not want me to take down our trees.

Then the neighbors said, "These church people are noisy. They bring a lot of people into our community with a lot of cars and commotion. We don't want them here."

The man who was chairman of the hearing sat there listening to them, and I did not say anything.

He dismissed the meeting, and I said, "I would like to see you in your office."

I went into his office, and he said, "Sit down," but I said, "I don't want to sit down."

So I leaned over toward him, and said, "You saw seventy-two people didn't you? I have come to tell you it would be better to sign the papers for our church. You see I can bring a thousand people down town to speak for our church.

He said, "Yes, I think you should have the church," and he signed them.

Some of those people who opposed our church have lost their jobs, some died of cancer, others moved away, and we have bought six of the houses that touch our property. Every one of them that comes up for sale, we purchase.

Most of those who came against our church are gone. There probably are not more than three or four of them left in the area. You cannot come against what God is doing and not reap what you sow.

There are times in this life when you not only have to let the devil know how you feel about something, you have to let people know how you feel.

You need to speak this way in every area of your life. Do not speak weakly and say silly things. Speak with strength.

If people say, "You're audacious," just tell them, "Well, it's for Jesus." Then go ahead. Do not back up on being strong in the Lord and the power of His might.

8

Give Militantly

As I was making this list of militant victorious positions for Christians to take, the Lord said to me, "People need to learn to give militantly. Dropping a dollar bill into the offering plate and tipping the waitress five dollars — that is nauseating to me. Tell them they need to learn to give militantly. If they give militantly, I'll bless them militantly."

During the time we were building our new church in South Bend, an evangelist came by to speak for us.

He said, "I need a truck to carry my tent. Would you buy a truck for me?"

And I said, "Well, yes, how much is it?"

He said, "Forty thousand dollars," and I wrote him out a check for that amount. There was only one problem — we didn't have the money. But I never did tell him so. We had some money in the building fund, and I took forty thousand dollars out of it, which slowed down the building process a little bit.

However, in my spirit, the Lord said, "He asked for it, give it to him."

So I gave it to him. We never did borrow any money for that church building. We just kept believing God until we got the thing up.

A few weeks later, a doctor from another city called and said he wanted to see me. I agreed, so he came over to our television station.

He said, "I like this station of yours, and I have an offering to give you. First, I have a story I want to tell you.

"When I came into this money, I wanted to give some of it to every one of the television evangelists, pastors and teachers on your station. It would have been a nice offering for each of them, but the Lord stopped me and said, 'You can't do that. You have to give it all to Brother Sumrall.'

"I said, Lord, I don't want to do that. I want to divide this among all of the programs on his station.

"But the Lord repeated, 'No, you have to give all of it to Brother Sumrall.' "

The doctor went to his wife and said, "Honey, would you pray about something? I won't tell you what it is, but will you pray for a couple of days, and I'll come back and talk to you."

Two days later, he said to her, "Did you pray?"

And she said, "Yes, but you won't like it."

"Why won't I like it?" he asked.

"The Lord told me that the money we received should all be given to Brother Sumrall, and that you wanted to give it to several pastors and evangelists," she said.

He answered, "Well, that's what I wanted you to pray about. The Lord told you the same thing He told me."

So he called me and made arrangements to bring over the check.

He said, "Here is the check, and I want you to know that God says you should have it to use for anything that you like. It's the Lord's money."

I looked, and it was a check for $150,000. So I prayed over the doctor and his wife. When they left, I did what you would have done. Who wouldn't?

But the Lord said, "Don't do that, don't do that."

I said, "Why not?"

He said, "If you had not given the missionary the forty thousand, I would not have given this money. I always give back more than I receive."

I said, "Oh, is that right?"

He said, "When you give energetically, I will give back to you energetically."

He had to fight the doctor in order to get that money to me, but God waged war until He got hold of the doctor and made him bring it all to me so that we could finish our church building. If you have the courage to give militantly, God will match your courage with blessing.

A Lesson Well-Learned

After we had the great revival in the Philippines, and many of those beautiful people came into the church, I taught on giving and faith to receive. In our congregation was a school teacher who was very energetic. We got to know her quite well.

One Sunday, the ladies who counted the offering brought me a check and said, "The high school teacher has put in her whole check."

So I took the check and went to see her.

I said, "Sister, there's been a little mistake here. Your entire check is in the offering. Are you sure that's what you meant to do?

She said, "Yes, I'm sure."

I said, "Oh, now, you are just out of the Roman Catholic Church, and I don't know how much they take. But we only take 10 percent."

She said, "I don't think it is any of your business what I give to God."

So I went and put it back in the offering. I did not think too much about it until the first of the next month when the ladies were counting the offering. There was a second check for the whole month — her entire paycheck. Well, I was a good pastor, so I went and got the check and told her to come see me.

I said, "This is the second month you have done this. We don't want you to starve. We want you to pay your rent. I want to give something back to you for this."

She looked at me real calmly and asked, "Do you do all your members this way? Try to give back their offerings?"

"No," I said, "only you."

She said, "Well, I give unto God what I want to, and it is none of your business."

So I said thank you and put her check back in the offering.

Everything went along fine for the next four weeks. Then when the ladies counted the offering, there was a third check from the school teacher, her whole salary for the month. Now I was angry. I did not talk to her out in the building but took her into my office.

"I want to tell you something," I said to her. "I don't want any disgrace on this church. I don't want anyone saying I am stealing money off of my people. Ten percent is a nice amount to give to God, and that's all we want you to give."

She began to cry and said, "I've never known anyone like you! I want to tell you something. In the past three months, I have had more money than I have ever had in my life. I have had more clothes than I have ever had in my life. I have had more food than I have ever had in my life, and I have had more joy than I have ever had in my life.

"If you will just leave me alone, God is bringing things into my life, spiritually and materially, beyond anything I have ever known. When I give to God, He gives back to me more than I have ever had before, and we are in a loving relationship that you would never believe could happen."

Some preachers are so dull, you know? They cannot even tell when God is moving in people's hearts. Here I was wanting to give it back, give it back, give it back, and she wanted to give and give and give. I did not realize God was doing a mighty work in that little Catholic lady's heart.

You Cannot Beat God at Giving

We must learn to give aggressively. I know that at first you are afraid to. Get fear out of your heart. God is a good God. I have tried His ways now for almost sixty years. If you give to Him, He will give back to you. Only His giving is so much greater than ours. He likes to grab something and just shake it, so He can put more in. He likes to give you more and then run over the top. He likes to fill the saucer as well as the cup.

We will come to a time in history when your real estate will not be worth anything. God is going to burn this earth one of these days, and your diamonds and gold will be valueless. The only thing that is going to leave Planet Earth is God's people.

You should be more interested in God's people than anything else. All of these other things are going to be consumed here. So be able to trade off anything you have for a blessing any time. You will find that giving aggressively to God will open doors of blessing to you.

I give aggressively, but not as much as some people I know. I am amazed at some people. They give so aggressively, it is almost frightening. Kenneth Copeland is one of the greatest givers on the face of the earth. I ride around in airplanes he has given away in Africa and Central America. Even after he has given ministries the planes, if they need repair, he will bring the planes back to America and have them repaired. He is one of the best men living on the face of the earth.

He gave me $100,000 not long ago for The End-time Joseph Program, and said, "You go feed those hungry people, and let me know about it."

I am careful to let him know, too. Every time we make a food delivery, I am very careful to make sure he knows about it. That man gives so furiously that God gives back to him furiously.

Give God a few little coins and a few little dollars, and you cannot get a lot out of Him. But if you will give to God generously, aggressively, you will find that there is a God up there Who likes that kind of giving. That is the kind of giver I want to be.

When I came back to this country at twenty-three years of age, after making a three-year missionary tour around the world, I told people I had found "gold mines."

I said, "I found gold mines in Singapore, in Bombay, in Shanghai, in Hong Kong, and in Manila. I could go there and drive a solid-gold Cadillac. Those people are givers."

The denominational "authorities" said, "Well, don't be telling anyone. You'll mess up our missionary program."

They did not want to believe me, but God has shown the church today that what I said was true. In a Third World country called Korea is the largest church on the face of the earth. Dr. Paul Yonggi Cho's Full Gospel Church in Seoul, Korea, has more than six hundred thousand members — all of them givers.

Rick Seaward in Singapore gives $1.5 million in American dollars each year to missions. I have gone to see him a couple of times a year, and I began to learn how he does it.

For example, here is a young girl, a typist, who makes $1,500 a month and gives half of it to missions. Then God blesses her for the other half. The most sacrificing people on the face of the earth are in that church in Singapore. It seats five thousand, and they have to have from three to five services every Sunday to accommodate the people.

It is no longer a time to sit back for the devil. It is no longer a time to whisper. Let the devil have it as if you were the lion. Let him know you are attached to the Lion of the Tribe of Judah and that everything he has is going to nothing. Everything we have is building up to Jesus. We have no fear because our leader is moving out aggresively in front of us.

The Man Who Kept 10 Percent

The late R.G. LeTourneau, manufacturer of those great earth-moving machines, was the foremost example of an aggressive giver that I know anything about.

I lived with him in his home years ago. We would sit around at night and talk. He lived in Peoria, Illinois, at that time. And he let me preach in his big factory, right during the top working hours.

He would call everyone in his factory together and say, "I'm paying your salary. Now, listen to Brother Sumrall."

And I would stand up there and preach away at them while they drew their salaries.

LeTourneau told me, "When I started in Stockton, California, in a little garage with my dad, I gave the Lord 10 percent because my daddy told me to. But I had not been doing this but a few months when I found I had too much left over. So I told God I would give Him 20 percent.

"I got along so well that I said, 'Lord, I might as well give you 30 percent. I still have a little too much.' A little later, I began to give the Lord 40 percent, because I continued to have more than I needed."

However, he learned an important lesson about giving during the depression years. One year, he made $35,000 profit. That year, he had made a pledge of $5,000 to his church in the Christian and Missionary Alliance denomination. But, puffed up with pride, he decided to withhold his pledge, reinvest it in the business, and pay it double the next year, when he expected to clear $100,000.[1]

Of course, his anticipated profit did not materialize. In fact, he faced a $100,000 loss! Thoroughly chastened, he made a pledge for the year he skipped plus the same pledge for the following year — even in the face of $100,000 worth of debts and no money for the payroll. Also, his bookkeeper was threatening to quit!

From that point on, his business turned around, and within four years, he and his wife founded the LeTourneau Foundation, made up of 90 percent of the stocks of LeTourneau Corporation, and those earnings financed Christian work worldwide.

He told me the time came when he said, "Lord, I am going to make my giving 50 percent. I am going to split what I make with you, seeing that you give me all the ideas that are making these millions of dollars."

One of his "ideas" resulted in those monster wheels that are taller than a man, and every wheel has a motor in it. If the machine has ten wheels on the ground, it has ten motors, and you cannot stick it in any mud on the face of the earth. His machines can move more dirt in a day than they used to move in a month.

Then he said, "Lord, I'd better give You 60 percent. I have too much left," and a little later, he said, "Lord, I'll make it 70 percent, if You don't mind."

He told me, "Brother Sumrall, I finally just decided the best thing was to give God 90 percent and keep the tenth for myself. Now, you know what my problem is? I still have so many millions in the bank, I do not know what to do with them!"

LeTourneau often said: "It is not how much money I give to God, but how much of God's money I keep for myself."

He told *Forbes* magazine: "I like to do two things. One is to design machines, turn on the power, and see them work. The other is to turn on the power of the Gospel and see it work in people's lives."[2]

At his death in 1969, he held more than two hundred patents for his inventions. He talked militantly and gave militantly.

If you say, "Yes, but that won't work for me," then it will not — you just said so with your own mouth. The truth is that God's principle of giving always works, no matter who is the giver or where he lives.

Hindrances To Receiving

Giving into bad ground will keep your harvest from materializing. Some people put their money into causes that they know are dead. They keep giving out of tradition or sympathy. Perhaps their parents and grandparents went to a church which was alive and moving for God, but now for some reason, the glory has departed. Your money will not grow in dead soil.

I used to give money a lot of times out of sympathy. I was a sympathetic giver. If your crocodile tears were bigger than someone else's, you got more out of me.

Then the Lord spoke to me and said, "That's not the way to give. The way for you to give is the pattern in Genesis 1 and 2, where I commanded everything to produce after its kind."

What you should do in your giving is reproduce yourself. If you are an evangelist, give to evangelism. If you are in the Word, give to Word teaching. Do not give to something opposite.

Years and years ago, I preached in a very large church in New York. The pastor was one of the strongest preachers in the nation. As I traveled around the world, I met many missionaries sent out from his church — but I never met one of them who could preach.

He was a big Irishman, a former policeman who stood six feet and four inches, and knew how to put his foot down right. When he got wound up, all of New York huddled, he was so fierce. When he got saved and became a preacher, they understood that a man of God was in town.

Yet all of his missionaries around the world could not teach a Sunday school class in his church, and he had sent them out. The Lord told us to reproduce after our own kind. If you love a certain area, build a church over there. Call another church in another country by the name of your church. See if you can transplant what is on the inside of you, then they will have the same spirit. Keep visiting there and see that they have the same spirit you have inside of you.

God wants all of us to give to that which is like us. We want to reach the world. Keep your heart on that. Do not give to something that is not going to save anything just because you feel sorry for them.

Our giving must be with the same attitude that governs the rest of our lives.

All of these winning positions affect your whole life. You even look like your decisions. Look in the mirror first thing in the morning and greet "Mr., Mrs., or Miss Decision." The decisions you make affect your facial expressions. Those little flat muscles underlying your skin look like they do today because of the way you have been holding your face.

Your decisions to give will cause your face to look inviting. You will have a "giving" face, one that people like to see coming toward them.

---

[1]Tan, *Encyclopedia of 7700 Illustrations*, pp. 474, 475.

[2]Ibid, p. 475.

9

Go Out Militantly

There were giants on the earth in those days . . . .
Genesis 6:4

The Bible says **There were giants on the earth in those days**...but there is much speculation among theologians and writers about these giants. We don't need to dispute among ourselves about who they were or their origin, suffice to accept what the Bible says — they existed. Elsewhere in the Old Testament we read of the giants on the earth who were fearful to behold and scared the wits out of otherwise sensible men.

I submit to you that there are "giants" on the earth today also — giants that are not ten feet tall, giants that don't sleep in thirteen feet long and six feet wide beds (see Deut. 3:11 NIV), but they are commanding in what they demand from those who succumb to them and their evil hold. The Bible tells us to kill these giants when we encounter them, but you don't do it by looking at their bigness. Giants are done away with by looking to your Source of strength. Giants can be defeated. Giants can be reduced to midgets incapable of harming you or your loved ones. But you can't play with giants of sin and rebellion or they will overpower and destroy you.

The evil giants in the Old Testament days were killed. You don't wound or just embarrass giants.

David's encounter with the giant Goliath teaches an indisputable truth. David said,

> "You come to me with a sword, with a spear, and and with a javelin. But I come to you in the name of the Lord of hosts, the God of the armies of Israel, whom you have defied.
>
> This day the Lord will deliver you into my hand, and I will strike you and take your head from you … that all the earth may know that there is a God in Israel.
>
> Then all this assembly shall know that the Lord does not save with sword and spear; for the battle is the Lord's, and He will give you into our hands"
>
> 1 Samuel 17:45-47

Whether it is fear, alcohol, drugs, festering hatreds, lust, or whatever the monster stalking you, you can be set free from that giant.

David didn't need Saul's armor, and you don't need someone else's armor either. You need to use what God has given you, but you need to know that it has to be used.

We are not to be giant offenders, we are to be giant killers. Jesus said in Acts 1:8, **But you shall receive power when the Holy Spirit has come upon you ….** We have been given that power to defeat the giants sent by the devil. One of the ways we do that is through going out militantly to our families, our neighbors, our cities and towns.

Many times people will witness apologetically, as if they are ashamed to stand up for what they believe. You do not apologize for saving someone from the fires of hell. That is where people are going who do not receive Jesus.

We are not to be apologetic or timid. We are to go out in the strength and power of the Lord.

This requires boldness. We have many biblical precedents for this. The Apostle Paul, writing to the Christians at Corinth, said, **Great is my boldness of speech toward you** ... (2 Cor. 7:4).

When writing to the Christians at Ephesus, Paul told them his only purpose in life was to **enlighten all men and make plain to them what is the plan [. . . for the salvation of all men] ... in [the person of] Christ Jesus our Lord; In Whom, because of our faith in Him, we dare to have the boldness (courage and confidence) of free access...** (Eph. 3:9a, 11b, 12a AMP).

In effect, he said the same thing when writing to the Christians at Phillipi (see Phil. 1:20), to Timothy (1 Tim. 3:13), and to the Christians at Rome (Rom. 15:5).

Whoever the writer of Hebrews was, he made the same kind of statements, saying, **Let us therefore come boldly to the throne of grace** (Heb. 4:16), and **so we may boldly say: "The Lord is my helper; I will not fear. What can man do to me?"** (Heb. 13:6).

When you study the book of Acts, you see with what boldness Peter, John and Paul spoke. They went out boldly, fearlessly disputing against the giants of religiosity of their day, standing up for what the Holy Spirit had revealed to them. There was never any compromise. And we know what happened. Thousands came into "the way" as a result of their witness.

Begin at Home

Begin at home. Militantly begin to get your family saved. Many parents pay little or no attention to their children until it is too late. Right under their noses, the kids just go to the devil.

They let their children have the wrong friends, bring the wrong music into the house, and watch the wrong television programs.

A parent says, "I do not know what's in my son's room."

What is wrong with that parent? Parents should know what that son has in his room and where it came from. Everything that is not of God should be gotten rid of. Children should be told that as long as they live in your house and eat at your table, wrong things are not going to be in your house. Otherwise, the blessing of God will not be on the house. In the past fifty years, we have lost fifty million young people because we did not go after them militantly in our own homes.

Why does a pastor have children in his home and lose them all to the devil? I do not understand that. I have three sons: one is business manager of our office, another is in charge of radio and television, and the third is a preacher. All my sons love the Lord. They all serve the Lord, and no one made them do it.

Perhaps you wonder why they are like that. It is because we brought them up in the nurture and admonition of the Lord. Our dining table was not a place where preachers were criticized.

Our dining table was not a place where they heard me say, "Oh, my, I am so tired of the ministry I don't know what to do. There are just too many people bearing down on me."

They never heard that kind of talk. When I left the church office at 5 p.m., I walked out the door and closed it. I kicked all the little demons in, and I said, "You stay there. I'll fight you tomorrow morning." Then I went home and had a good time.

I did not go home griping to my wife who was fixing me a good dinner, telling her what a hard time I had that day. Many preachers tell too much to their wives. Wives have their own problems. They have their own burdens. Why should they have to bear their husbands' also? Some ministers' wives are having nervous breakdowns, because they are bearing more burdens than they ought to be.

So my boys grew up as a family in a house where we had fun together. We rolled on the floor and wrestled together. We played golf and went swimming together. Even in Manila, even in Hong Kong, even in Jerusalem, we would go to the nearest water and go swimming together. We ate together.

I did not have to tell them the burdens I was bearing. That was between me and God. Preachers and their wives need to learn to take their burdens to Jesus. He is the Burden Bearer. You do not have to carry your own burdens.

Go after your immediate family. Get your father saved, your mother, your aunt and uncle. Go after them.

You say, "Oh, they won't like it."

It does not matter whether they like it or not. It is better than going to hell.

You say, "They won't like me."

It does not matter whether they like you or not. They may not anyway. What difference does it make, compared to their going to hell?

Your Community

Go after your community militantly. When Peter and John were taken into custody for healing the sick, performing miracles, teaching the people and preaching about Jesus' resurrection from the dead, they were asked, "By what power or by what name have you done this?"

Peter, filled with the Holy Spirit, cried out, **"Let it be known to you all, and to all the people of Israel, that by the name of Jesus Christ of Nazareth, whom you crucified, whom God raised from the dead, by Him this man stands here before you whole..."** (Acts 4:10). He told them there was salvation in none other. The Bible faithfully records the reaction of the religious council and the people: **Now when they saw the boldness of Peter and John, and perceived that they were uneducated and untrained men, they marveled. And they realized that they had been with Jesus** (v. 13).

Have you ever stopped to think what would have happened to the first century Church if Peter and John had been afraid to speak up in Jerusalem, their community?

Your community is important to God because of its people. The cities in your state are important to God.

Satan wants to gain control of the government, of the legislature, the law enforcement officers. Look at the inroads Satan has made in our educational institutions. Kids in school have satanist clubs. Bible clubs are banned, but satanist clubs flourish. Witchcraft flourishes. We are facing a powerful foe.

There can be no lone rangers in this kind of spiritual warfare. You need to be involved in the civic activities of your community or city. One of the most aggressive members of my church is on the city council. And she's a lady!

You need to be making your city God-conscious. There are satanic strongholds that need to be pulled down.

Have you heard the media refer to "the soul of the city?" Cities don't have souls; people do. But cities are like persons absorbing the personality of those who live there. You can bless your city through your participation in events that shape the direction your city (or community) goes. Your thoughts, words, civic-mindedness, pride — or condemnation and neglect, the opposites of the good things that can build up or tear down a city.

There are many wounded and unloved cities across our land. There are many cities with a dark soulish cloud hovering over them.

We have some biblical examples of men who made a difference in their cities. Jesus Himself wept over Jerusalem. Nehemiah wept, prayed and fasted over the same city in his day. Daniel was thrown in a lions' den because of his commitment to Jerusalem. **Mockers** [scornful men and women] **stir up a city, but wise men turn away anger** (Prov. 29:8 NIV). Cities are important to God. You community matters to Him.

How do you take a city? You can march, write letters to the editor — you can do any of all the things the Constitution gives you the right to do — but there's something more important than laying on the sidewalk in front of abortion clinics and going to jail. Breaking the law is a way to show strong protest and has been proven to call attention to the views of those protesting. We need people to protest, to write letters, to march, to speak up and say what's in their hearts. Don't sit still and do nothing. But we need to do more — we need to love the people in our cities and communities. We need to show them the love of God in Christ Jesus. Our churches need to be strong in our communities, lighthouses reflecting all that is good, right and moral.

You can either antagonize the heart of your city so that it becomes your enemy, or you can become its friend. You can help to feed the hungry, contribute to the needs of the homeless, make friends with civic leaders, show appreciation to the law enforcement agencies in your community, let your presence be seen and felt at the hospitals, retirement centers, and provide a haven for spiritual refreshment.

Civil action by itself will produce strife; spiritual warfare moves on a higher plane. It will involve much prayer and putting into action the principles outlined in this book. It means holding to biblical truth in winsome ways. The Great Commission handed to us by Jesus Himself was to preach the Gospel, not to fight the devil by being obnoxious. We are in a fight, but it is a battle for biblical truth. Let us be faithful to our calling, exhibitions of the grace of God, demonstrating by our lifestyle that we are "called-out ones" mighty through God.

We don't need clever techniques; we do need to fight the good fight using our spiritual weapons, boldly proclaiming the resurrection message.

Building a Church Militantly

When I went to the Philippines, I frightened everyone. As I wrote earlier, we bought a B-52 hangar and began to establish a church, and we did not even have five people.

Someone from a Bible society came to visit and said, "What are you going to do here?"

I said, "I'm building a church."

This man's office and big Bible store was only a two-minute walk from me.

He said, "Well, sir, this building will hold half the Protestants in town."

I said, "Fairly soon, not one tenth of the Protestants in town will be able to get in here."

He asked, "What do you think you are going to do to accomplish that?"

"Get them saved," I answered.

"Oh," he said, "I've heard other people say that."

I said, "Well, now you've heard another one say it."

He seemed kind of upset and said, "You're going to go out and take everyone else's church members and

89

bring them over here, and all the other churches will be emptied."

"No," I said, "we're going to fill up those empty churches you are talking about."

Then I looked at him — a great, big guy — and said, "I would like to prophesy to you please. My prophecy is this: Within a few months time, you will not have a single Bible for sale because of the revival God is going to give."

In the natural, it looked as if I was talking crazy. I was building a place to seat two thousand people when I did not have five yet. He was looking at natural things, but I was looking with the eye of faith.

God had said, "If you will build it, I'll fill it."

My part was just to build the thing. That hangar had never been put up. I found it in a storage place, bought it very cheaply, and I was putting it up.

Not long afterward, God did send us that mighty revival where 150,000 people came to the Lord.

I said to them, "Go buy yourself a Bible at the Bible Bookstore."

Later, I walked into his store and said, "Have you got a Bible?"

"No, sir, I don't," he said, "We have sent to London and told them to ship Bibles out by air. For the first time in our history, we don't have a single Bible for sale."

I tell you, reader, you can do what you want to do. You must get the "want to" in your heart. You can do it if you go out militantly, determined to win or to accomplish what God has set you to do.

Anytime you set out to do something in an easy way, you are not going to be a victor. This is a time of victory. Whatever we do, we are going to do it militantly, in the name of Jesus.

A Loss of Militancy

When I was a young man, I went around the world preaching. By the age of twenty-six, what became World War II was already raging in Europe, and I was chased out. Then I preached in every large church of a certain denomination in this country, from New York to the West Coast.

Today, few of those churches are of any value to anyone. Why? They stopped going out militantly. They are all dead. I cannot fathom that, yet it happened. Those great missionary churches are hardly anything today. They are down to almost zero attendance.

Why do churches flourish and then die?

Why do denominations die?

I believe one big reason is that they stop going out militantly. They forget the Great Commission (Matt. 16:15,16) and turn inward. They become little "bless-me" clubs, places of habit and tradition, places of custom.

The major denominations in this country have withdrawn a large percentage of their total missionary personnel in the past ten years. The missionary force of the world is coming out of the Word of Faith movement right now. Those young men and women are going out in mighty strength, power, determination, and audacity toward the devil. Thank God for it in Jesus' name.

In a report given to a missionary conference in 1900, this was said:

> If there were only one Christian in the world, and he worked and prayed a year to win one friend to Christ, and if these two then continued each year to win one more, and if every person thus led into the kingdom led another to Christ every year, in thirty-one years every person in the world would be won for Christ.[1]

Sad to say, Christians in 1900 did not do that, and the world is yet unwon to Christ.

Today, it is imperative that we go militantly and begin to bring in the harvest. If each reader of this book wins at least one person to Christ in the year after reading this, it will make a difference. Then encourage that new convert to go out and win one.

Spiritual Famine and Poverty

The Father is yearning to have all of His children with Him. He wants us to finish the work He has set for the Church. He wants us to go militantly and win as many lost souls for Him as possible. He wants us to evangelize militantly.

Worldwide missionary efforts by Protestants really began about 1815 and did not get truly under way until the mid-nineteenth century. Missions flourished until World War I, then began to drop off. After the

Pentecostal movement spread through this country, there was another wave of missions throughout the world. Again a war seemed to stop this move.

Since the 1940s, there has been a lessening of missionary interest in the Western World. More mission efforts are being carried out today by Third World countries to Third World countries than from the West.

An expert on evangelization says that between the days of the early Church to 1885, some 200 schemes to evangelize the world had been tried and fizzled out, usually within ten or so years. He says that in the last hundred years, another one hundred schemes have been tried. Today, there are about fifty plans for global evangelization, and several of those are fading.[2]

In 1900, it was estimated that some 788 million people had not heard of Christ. Today, there are an estimated 1,300 million who have not heard the Gospel. Spiritual poverty is spreading faster than the Good News that man can be reconciled to God through Christ.

What does "the Great Commission" mean?

> And He said to them, "Go into all the world and preach the gospel to every creature.
>
> He who believes and is baptized will be saved; but he who does not believe will be condemned."
> **Mark 16:15,16**

When Jesus spoke this to His disciples, He was simply reiterating the Father's commands to Adam and Eve in Genesis 1:28: "Go forth to every part of the world and fill it with my glory."

Then God blessed them, and God said to them, "Be fruitful and multiply; fill the earth and subdue it . . . ."

If Adam and Eve had not sinned, today the world would be filled with the children of God, living in happiness, prosperity, and great harmony with their Father. Instead, we have unhappiness, poverty, and disharmony between God and His creation.

However, God's purpose has never changed, because He never changes. His purpose is still to have a world filled with His children, even if He has to make a new heaven and a new earth. (2 Pet. 3:13.) In the meantime, the Church has not fulfilled the Great Commission given by Jesus, and it still remains to be done.

God will not be defeated; therefore, His spiritual food and His Good News must be taken throughout the world before Jesus returns. We will not accomplish that without going out militantly and aggressively.

The disciples went out with authority and power. They were reaching the known world of their day (Col. 1:6,23) and were credited with turning the world upside down. (Acts 17:6.) However, even in their day, not every person had been able to hear the Word.

For the first time in history, radio and television make it possible for every person to hear the Gospel — if Christians will go out militantly or give militantly to missions work.

We can provide spiritual food to the hungry of the world.

Enemies of Militancy

Two of the greatest enemies of militant Christianity are apathy and complacency.

Apathy does not care whether anyone is saved or not. This attitude causes a Christian not to have any remorse over those who are going to hell. To be apathetic is to have or show little or no feeling or emotions, it is lack of concern, indifference. It is to be spiritless. This is the spirit that keeps people from making the effort to witness to others — a "don't care" attitude.

Complacency says, "I'm okay. I have gained heaven. Let someone else go out militantly. I am not called to be a missionary. It is someone else's problem, someone else's call, someone else's job." To be complacent is to be self-satisfied.

Perhaps you are thinking, "I'm too young," or "I'm too old." Not everyone can go to a foreign mission field. Not everyone is called to that. However, American society today is about as pagan as many places in any overseas country! Go to your neighborhood. Knock on doors. Give people the Good News that there is hope for their lives.

There are days when I feel I am just getting started for the Lord! I am like Moses, ready to enter into my third dimension with God. You had better watch me at eighty. I will be dangerous to the devil!

Our government's concept that men and women are ready to be put out to pasture at age sixty-five is alien to any previous cultures and to other countries. In the eastern part of the world, age is considered a sign of wisdom. Now, just when a man gets to know something, they want to put him out with the cows. Just when his abilities are keen, he has to leave the active world.

Industries are losing billions of dollars because they are releasing people who are just ready to teach the world something. The last years of life ought to be the best. People are no longer seeking to get something. They already have experienced life.

If even those retired Christians would get the vision of Moses and go forth to make their remaining years count for God, many souls could be won for the Kingdom. Even in retirement homes, a militant attitude for Christ will bring in rewards.

[1]Winter, Ralph D., and Hawthorne, Steven C., Editors. *Perspectives on the World Christian Movement, a Reader; The Missionary Problem is a Personal One* by Andrew Murrary (Pasadena: William Carey Library, The Institute of International Studies, 1981), p. 829.

[2]All missions information is taken from David B. Barrett's *Evangelize! A Historical Survey of the Concept,* The AD 200 Series (Birmingham: New Hope, 1987).

10

Resist the Enemy Militantly

The sixth attitude that I want you to have is to resist the enemy militantly. Let me give you an example: Suppose I was preaching, and a great big puppy wandered in and came up to sit on the platform. If I looked at him and said, "Puppy, get out of here," do you know what he would do? He would just wag his tail.

But if I turned around and yelled, "Get out!" he would skedaddle. My attitude and voice would be militant, and he would know I meant it.

Until you know how to tell the devil to get out, he is not going anywhere. You have to have the power of Jesus within you like a storm brewing, so that when you speak, that power goes out there and moves anything that is moveable. If you do that, God will bless you.

The Armor of a Christian

The devil is hard of hearing. If you do not talk loud, he cannot hear you at all. So we have to let him have it.

The best way to be able to resist the devil is to have on the full armor of God as discussed earlier in this book, and then to use all these weapons of our warfare.

The key scripture for this, of course, is Ephesians 6, beginning in verse 11 where we are told to:

> **Put on the whole armor of God, that you may be able to stand against the wiles of the devil.**
>
> **For we do not wrestle against flesh and blood, but against principalities, against powers, against the rulers of the darkness of this age, against spiritual hosts of wickedness in the heavenly places.**
>
> **Therefore take up the whole armor of God, that you may be able to withstand in the evil day, and having done all, to stand** (vv. 11-13).

This doesn't say to put on half of the armor, or a little bit of the armor. The Apostle Paul was inspired to write **put on the whole armor.** It is so necessary to have on all of the armor of God.

The first two words of verse 11 direct us to a responsibility: "Put on." In other words, God is not going to put it on for you. You put on the armor of God. You clothe yourself in strength and in might.

Perhaps you may say, "Why should I put on the whole armor of God?"

You put it on in order not to be defeated.

You put it on in order not to fall down, but to be able to stand.

You put it on in order to be the person God wants you to be.

Instead of saying, "Well, I'm licked. I'm whipped. I'm burned out," you will be able to withstand the storms of life.

Most people that are burned out have never been on fire. They "froze" out. They do not even know what the word "burned out" means. You do not burn out in God's work. You just grow brighter.

> **Your word is a lamp to my feet and a light to my path.**
> **Psalm 119:105**

> **I have taught you in the way of wisdom;**
> **I have led you in right paths.**
> **When you walk, your steps will not be hindered,**
> **And when you run, you will not stumble.**
> **Proverbs 4:11,12**

The paths of the righteous just grow brighter and brighter. When you are not growing brighter, you get colder and colder — God's icebergs — but even those can be warmed up. When an "iceberg melts," down inside such a Christian is the germ of eternal life that can be ignited to start a fire burning again.

Also, we are to put on the whole armor for "standing abilities." The **wiles of the devil** are his tricks, his maneuverings. In the years to come, the devil will have a lot of new tricks, a lot of other temptations. We need to have on the whole armor so that whatever the devil has been saving for these last times will not affect us.

Be certain you have on all of the armor Paul mentions so that you resist the enemy militantly.

When the Bible says to be vigilant, the writers meant for us to see what Satan is doing in the world, to keep up with him, to resist and fight him in whatever way is necessary.

For example, the night I finally heard what had been happening in Bilibid Prison, Manila, for three weeks, I resisted the devil all night in prayer.

I prayed and wept in intercession for the city, for the girl, and for myself. I prayed because I was living in a place that had a great need, and I had not been helping to meet that need. I had been about the Lord's business of building a place for the harvest of a revival.

However, I was so busy with that one aspect that I had not been busy about the spiritual needs, or about spiritual warfare, about actively resisting the devil.

The next morning, the Lord sent me to deal with the situation, to cast the devil out of the girl. I did not want to go, but God assured me He had no one else to send. Therefore I went, and I have told you already about the door it opened for revival.

However, the point I want to make here is that gaining ground for God started with militant resistance in prayer and then in action. In order to be prepared for resistance, certain hindrances must be overcome.

Hindrances to Militant Resistance

Two of the major hindrances are worry and fear.

In my *How To Cope Series* is a little booklet on *Worry.* In it, I told of an incident that occurred years ago in Tibet, and I wrote:

> Your problems are no greater than those of any other person, and they are not too big for God to handle. So you should not become anxious or worried about them. Worry will only distort the true and

honest situation, making it seem much worse than it actually is.

You must reach down inside yourself, bring yourself up, and say, "Wait a minute. I'll not permit my spiritual being to become disturbed by this thing. That is not honorable and not right."

. . . Once many years ago, I was captured in Tibet by the Communists . . . As I was leading a caravan of seventeen people over the mountaintops, preaching the Gospel in the isolated villages, three armed men ambushed us and took us captive. They marched us along the rocky, treacherous mountain trails for about three hours.

The man who was guarding me was a grim, mean-looking fellow. He held his gun — one of those long-barreled Kentucky rifles — about six inches from the back of my head with his finger glued to the trigger. Had he stumbled on a rock, I would have been in trouble!

As we moved along, I knew the devil wanted to destroy me. I had to find a way out of that desperate situation if I wanted to go on living and breathing.

It was certainly time to be militant, but also a time to be wise! So I talked to the Lord in my heart.

I said, "Lord, these men have marched us for miles so they can kill us and take our cooking utensils and money. Have I come to Tibet to die?"

The Lord answered, "No."

"Then give me a promise to stand on."

"Revelation 19:6," The Lord came back. "Read it."

I always carried a New Testament with me, so I reached into my pocket and took it out. That verse says: **And I heard as it were the voice of a great multitude, and as the voice of many waters and as the voice of**

**mighty thunderings, saying, "Alleluia: for the Lord
God omnipotent reigneth"** (KJV).

These words caught me: "Alleluia: for the Lord
God omnipotent reigneth." The Word of God took away
all my anxiety. I turned around, I looked that man right
in the face, and laughed out loud. He became so
embarrassed and ashamed that he dropped the barrel
of his rifle toward the ground.

Through my interpreter I asked him, "Sir, why
don't you tell me what you want?"

He spoke up and said, "I'm hungry."

"Well, we'll feed you. We have a mule here loaded
with vegetables. We'll give you what you want."

"I need money," he added.

"We will give you money," I told him. "You don't
have to act like this."

So he took our vegetables and our money,
and trekked off into the forest with his two com-
panions.[1]

When we got to a village later that day, people told
us our release was a miracle. They told us that those
men were bandits who needed our animals and
everything else we had. It was a miracle we were not
killed. The miracle occurred because of militant
resistance to the devil's plans.

As I have said before, the first step in getting rid
of worry is "to know that you know that you know"
that He is in charge. The shield of faith will dispatch
worry.

Other places, I have written that fear is a Christian's
deadliest enemy. And I have told many times of my

strongest bout with fear as a seventeen-year-old called preacher.

My own father forbade me to leave home on a preaching tour, because he did not think I could make a living, and he had already spent money on educating me for a career. Then he walked out the door, pointed a finger at me, and said he expected me to be at home when he returned.

His unbending attitude struck fear to my heart. As I was weeping bitterly, that inner voice of divine guidance — the Holy Spirit — spoke to me to read Isaiah 41:10,11 (KJV), which begins with these words: **Fear thou not.**

Each phrase of those verses witnessed to my situation as if Isaiah had been writing just to me. Since then I have faced many fearful situations in my life, and only by God's grace and militant resistance, did I not fall prey to fear.

Fear brings spiritual poverty to the soul. For a healthy spiritual life, you must resist fear. Remember:

> **Greater is He that is in you, than he that is in the world.**
>
> **1 John 4:4**

[1]Sumrall, Lester. *Worry, How to Copy Series* (Tulsa: Harrison House, Inc., 1983), pp. 15-18.

11
Love Militantly

The seventh winning position in God's army is to love militantly.

We must love with force, with power, with authority. We must not love with "puppy love," but militantly. Let something flow out of you that is strong. Love aggressively.

Some people would not shake your hand, unless you stretch your hand out first. Some people will not speak to you, unless you speak first. God wants us to love with strength. He wants us to be aggressive with our love to the whole world.

Wherever you go, say, "God loves you, and I love you," and do not just say it. Mean it.

Love Is a Choice, a Decision, Not a Feeling.

"Feelings" or emotions are the result of love, not love itself. The world — as it does in almost everything — has distorted truth, facts, and principles of God. The world focuses on feelings, not reality. So when the feeling changes or leaves, as it certainly will, people think they do not love one another any longer.

Feelings alone do not weather life's challenges.

God so loved the world (John 3:16) enough to send His only begotten Son to ransom mankind. The Father made a choice, a decision. It was an act of His will. When we say we love someone, usually it is because we feel an emotion toward that person. Then, if that person no longer feeds our needs or triggers our emotions, we think love has left.

Actually, more than likely, love was never there. What was there was a physical or emotional need that was being met by the other person. We did not "love" them for themselves. We loved them for ourselves, for self-centered motives, because they made us "feel" good.

But real love always wins. When nothing else works in a situation, make a quality decision to love that person, and see the situation change. You cannot make that decision, of course, without forgiving that person or group (where forgiveness is necessary).

That is why the Lord advised us not to bring gifts to Him with unforgiveness, "un-love," in our hearts toward others. Lack of love toward our fellow man blocks the flow of love toward God.

Love Always Wins

I was holding a two-week meeting once in Hot Springs, Arkansas, in a certain church and was staying with the pastor at his home. About the second night, we were having a little dessert by the fire, because it was wintertime.

The pastor said to me, "Brother Sumrall, I have to close this meeting Sunday night."

I said, "I beg your pardon?"

"I have to close the meeting Sunday night," he repeated. Then he added, "My head deacon doesn't like you."

At that point, I didn't even know who the head deacon was!

The pastor said, "He told me to close this meeting Sunday night, that he could not stand you."

Inside, I became furious. It did not matter personally whether the man liked me or not, but I had a witness from the Holy Spirit that I was to be there two weeks. There were things the Lord wanted done, and this man was going to hinder the meeting simply because he did not like me?

I said, "I do not have anywhere to go next week. I was to be here for two weeks. I don't know what I would do."

The pastor said, "Well, that's your problem. The head deacon says it is all over. The meeting is to be closed."

I went to my room muttering inside to myself, wishing I could find that deacon and tell him a thing or two. Then the Lord spoke to me.

He said, "I want to tell you what to do. When you get to church tomorrow night, ask for him (the head deacon), go up to him, hug and kiss him."

I said, "Not on your life. No!"

The Lord said, "You do not really want revival here then, do you?"

Yes," I said, "I do."

He said, "Then go up to him, hug, and kiss him."

Some assignments from the Lord are kind of hard! I did not tell the pastor what I had heard from God, but the next night at church, I asked to be shown the head deacon. He was a little, old, scrawny thing who did not weigh ninety-eight pounds. If he had been bigger, I would have felt better about it.

But I spotted him, and I almost had to run him down, because he was trying to avoid me, of course. I grabbed him, and I hugged him, and I kissed him on the cheek.

I said, "God bless you, brother. I love you."

Believe me, that was loving by decision. That was speaking by faith. That was making a choice because of instructions from the Lord. I certainly had no "feelings" of love. Hugging him that night was like hugging a telephone pole. He made no response, not even a grunt.

After the service, back at the pastor's home, I said, "Lord, it's amazing how wrong You can be. That did not work."

He said, "Oh, yes, it worked, and you are to do that again tomorrow night."

I said, "Oh, no!"

He said, "Yes! Tomorrow night, if you are going to have revival."

I said, "Well, if that is the price of revival, I will pay it."

The next night, I had to chase the deacon again. He was there with a group of men. I went for him, hugged and kissed him, and again said, "God bless you, brother. I love you."

It was just like hugging an iceberg.

I said, "God, this does not work. This is not the way to do it."

But He said, "Yes, it is, and you have to do it again tomorrow night."

"Oh," I answered, "don't tell me I have to do this again!"

The Lord said, "It is working. Isn't it amazing that it's working, and you do not know it?"

The next night, I obeyed the Lord again for the sake of revival. I would not have done it for any other reason. I got hold of him, hugged him, kissed him, and said, "God bless you, brother. I love you." I did not hug or kiss anyone except the deacon.

That night, we got back to the pastor's home and were sitting around the fireplace eating dessert, and the pastor said, "Brother Sumrall, how long can you stay with us?"

I said, "Until Sunday."

He said, "Why don't you just stay longer?"

"Because," I answered, "your head deacon does not want me to stay longer."

"Well, I'll tell you," the pastor answered, "my deacon came around to me after church tonight and said, 'Pastor, I was mistaken. This is the best preacher we ever had in the history of this church.' "

It only took three hugs and kisses to accomplish that. Three little kisses on the cheek. Love always wins. Love can be aggressive.

If someone draws a circle and leaves you out, draw a bigger circle, and bring him in.

If someone says bad things about you, then say something good about him. Send him something nice.

The reason is that God is on the throne, Jesus is ruler of all things, and human beings can be changed through the working of the Holy Spirit.

In our communtiy, people did not think too highly of us in the beginning. They did not believe we would be able to build what has been established there. They did not believe we would ever get a television station on the air. But agape kept after them, you see.

Agape: Divine Love

In ancient, classical Greek, only three words were used for love. They were *eros,* which by the time of Jesus had come was associated only with physical, sensual feelings; *storge,* which means the kind of affection felt among family members; and *phileo,* a friendly affection.

Agape was first used in the Greek *Septuagint,* the first translation of the Hebrew scriptures (our Old Testament books) into any other language. About three hundred years before Jesus, Greek already was becoming a common language. So many Jews lived in foreign cities where mainly Greek was spoken that Jewish scholars in Alexandria, Egypt, made a translation into Greek.

However, in the *Septuagint*, the word *agape* was only used for God's love toward man. Greek scholars say that agape was a new word in the sense of its common usage in the cradle of New Testament Christianity. It means non-emotional love that is a deliberate choice, love by an act of the will.

Love without giving is not love. John 3:16 says that **God so loved** *(agape)* **the world that He gave.** This is the kind of love we are to have one for another — love that gives to the other what the other needs, not love that demands from another what you need.

We must give of ourselves in love, and if we will do that, we will be wonderful winners and victors in the Lord Jesus Christ.

The Lord spoke to me recently these words:

Be aggressive. Don't stand back. Don't be weak. Push forward. Reveal My greatness and My majesty. Reveal My love, and pour it on. Let them see that you mean it.

If someone preaches or even witnesses about the Lord, and people cannot tell if he means it or if what he is saying is real in his life, then people are not drawn to the Lord. You have to talk about the love of God with meaning.

God wants us to love our cities, our states, our nation, and the world — not the systems of this earth, not society, but the people of the world.

Reveal the Love of God

Once in my missionary travels around the world, I was in mainland China. In the primitive place where we were preaching, there were only little benches to sit on. The people were singing, and I was sitting on the front bench by my interpreter when a little street boy came in.

All he had on was a piece of cloth tied around his waist and covering the lower portion of his body. Otherwise, his entire body was naked. He slept in the alleys. He was so dirty, just crusted with dirt.

But he came in and sat by me, and he was looking up at all that singing. I do not know why I did this, except that it is natural to reach out to children. I put my arm around him, took him by the ear and shook it a little bit, and smiled at him.

He had not seen many white men, I am sure, but he turned around and smiled back. So we sat there together, and every so often I would look down and smile at him. I also would pat his shoulder.

And he turned to my interpreter and said, "This man loves me, doesn't he?"

At that point, to be honest, I did not love him. He was a dirty, street boy whom I had never seen. I cannot tell you why I hugged him and touched him, except I do all little boys that way. When I patted him on the shoulder, he was just another human being.

But when the interpreter told me what he said, my spirit opened, and I said, "Yes, I love you. I do love you."

The Lord brought love to life inside me in response to that little boy's need.

There are many places in the Bible that talk of love: love of God for man, man for God, and man for man. The most well-known, of course is the thirteenth chapter of the Apostle Paul's first epistle to the Corinthians. In that chapter, he tells what love is and what real *agape* love is not.

Love in the Word

There are a number of places where other inspired writers also tell us what love is. One of those places is 1 John 4.

We know God through love, the Apostle says:

> Beloved, let us love on another, for love is of God; and everyone who loves is born of God and knows God.
>
> He who does not love does not know God, for God is love.
>
> In this the love of God was manifested toward us, that God has sent His only begotten Son into the world, that we might live through Him.
>
> In this is love, not that we loved God, but that He loved us and sent His Son to be the propitiation for our sins.
>
> Beloved, if God so loved us, we also ought to love one another.
>
> 1 John 4:7-11

Also, we can see God through love:

> No one has seen God at any time. If we love one another, God abides in us, and His love has been

perfected in us. [We can know God exists because we see His love in us and in others for one another.]

By this we know that we abide in Him, and He in us, because He has given us of His Spirit.

And we have seen and testify that the Father has sent the Son as Savior of the world.

Whoever confesses that Jesus is the Son of God, God abides in him, and he in God.

And we have known and believed the love that God has for us. God is love; and he who abides in love abides in God, and God in him (vv. 12-16).

The result of love, John says in this chapter, is boldness, lack of fear, and obedience. Therefore, you can see that if we love with the love of God it brings militancy and an aggressiveness in obeying His commandments.

Love has been perfected among us in this: that we may have boldness in the day of judgment; because as He is, so are we in this world.

There is no fear in love; but perfect love casts out fear, because fear involves torment. But he who fears has not been made perfect in love.

We love Him, because He first loved us.

If someone says, "I love God," and hates his brother, he is a liar; for he who does not love his brother whom he has seen, how can he love God whom he has not seen?

And this commandment we have from Him: that he who loves God must love his brother also.

1 John 4:17-21

Loving others and loving God with His divine love is not optional for a Christian: It's a command. And,

I believe, according to the verses above and other scriptures, that if you are not loving militantly, then you are really not loving at all.

If we need to, let's change our attitudes and move strongly into the area of militant love.

12

Seven Losing Positions

If you do not want to be a winner, here are seven attitudes, or "battle positions," that will cause you to be a loser. Hang onto these, and you will not have victory in your life. You certainly will not be able to move out militantly.

Number One: Unbelief

The first is unbelief, to be unbelieving, to have doubt and disbelief.

A losing attitude says, "Oh, God can't do that," or "God won't do that."

You might have a losing attitude at work, and bring it into your home; you might have a losing attitude at home and take it into your work.

Some people would like to bring an attitude of unbelief into my church, but I keep casting that losing spirit out of there. We have seventeen double doors in the church, and when I say, "Scat! Get out of here," I mean it!

We are going to have faith in God. We are not going to have an unbelieving attitude. The Bible demonstrates that unbelief is lack of faith. We are told that Jesus was unable to **do many works of power there** [Capernaum],

**because of their unbelief — their lack of faith [in the
divine mission of Jesus]** (Matt. 13:58 AMP).

On one occasion the disciples were seeking to cast
out a demon from an epileptic, but were having no
success. The father of the boy brought him to Jesus who
rebuked the demon, and it came out of him, and the
boy was cured instantly. Then the disciples asked Jesus
why they couldn't drive it out, and Jesus said to them,
Because of the littleness of your faith [your unbelief]
**— that is, your lack of firmly relying trust. For truly,
I say to you, if you have faith [that is living] like a
grain of mustard seed, you can say to this mountain,
Move from here to yonder place, and it will move, and
nothing will be impossible to you** (Matt. 17:20 AMP).

Jesus marveled because of the unbelief He
encountered (Mark 6:6.) Following His resurrection and
appearance unto the two men walking on the Emmaus
road, and to the eleven disciples, He reproved them,
rebuking them for their unbelief and lack of faith and
their stubborn refusal to believe those who had seen
Him after He had risen. (Mark 16:14.)

We do well to pay attention to what disturbed
Jesus. Unbelief indicates hardness of heart. That does
not please God. The Lord confirmed the word with
signs and miracles following (Mark 16:20) when the
disciples demonstrated belief and faith.

Unbelief will keep you from preaching the Gospel,
from operating in the gifts of the Spirit, from casting
out demons or speaking with new tongues. Certainly,
you will not lay hands on the sick to recover if you
operate in unbelief.

You will not win any battles for the Lord from a position of unbelief.

Number Two: Self-Centeredness

It is so easy, you know, to let all your attention go inside yourself, good or bad.

"I am this, and I am that, and I am there. I am sad, and I am rejected. I am angry," or "I am happy."

We do not have to be self-centered. We need to be God-centered. That will cause our focus to be on meeting the needs of others, on letting the love and mercy of the Lord flow out of us to the hurt, wounded, and hungry ones of the world.

The devil would like to keep us "contemplating our navels" as the eastern religions do. He would like us to wear our feelings on our shoulders, so that we can be offended or rejected at every little thing. If he cannot do that, he will try to cause us to focus on our bodies through sicknesses or disease, through addictions to food or drink, or through an over-emphasis on sex.

Many Christians do not realize they are self-centered, because they do not have an emotional or body focus. Yet, they are selfish when they run from meeting to meeting to get blessed instead of settling down where God tells them to and becoming a worker for the Kingdom.

The Apostle Paul cautioned against this: **For the time will come when they will not endure sound doctrine, but according to their own desires, because they have itching ears, they will heap up for themselves**

teachers; and they will turn their ears away from the truth, and be turned aside to fables (2 Tim. 4:3,4).

Today, with the abundance of churches, television and radio programs, and seminars, it is possible to be spiritually self-centered. There is nothing wrong with attending meetings and tuning in Christian programs. However, if all of your time is spent taking in spiritual food and constantly seeking some new revelation — some "tasty morsel" of spiritual food that is new and different — then you are focusing on yourself.

The fivefold ministry was established by Jesus to perfect the saints (Eph. 4:11,12) to do the work of the ministry, not to sit and get fat or just maintain themselves. The *work of the ministry* is the Great Commission:

> And He said to them, "Go into all the world and preach the gospel to every creature.
>
> "He who believes and is baptized will be saved; but he who does not believe will be condemned.
>
> "And these signs will follow those who believe: In My name they will cast out demons; they will speak with new tongues;
>
> "they will take up serpents; and if they drink anything deadly, it will by no means hurt them; they will lay hands on the sick, and they will recover."
> Mark 16:15-18

Number Three: Being Conformed to This World

Most of the Church today is worldly. Christians watch worldly — even ungodly — television programs and movies. Christians put their money in the state lotteries and play Bingo. It seems many people are equating legality with spirituality. If the government says it is legal, then Christians feel it is okay to allow pornography ("free" speech), gambling, and even murdering unborn babies (abortion).

In America today, what is legal is not always right, and what is illegal is not always wrong. Government sanctions are no substitute for God's morality.

Until we can say, "I am not of this world but of another;" until we, like Abraham, can be a pilgrim and stranger through this world's systems, we are not going to be effective for the Kingdom of God.

The earth is the Lord's with all of its resources, but the world's system is not of the Lord. We belong on this planet. God created it for man to live on and enjoy. However, the systems that still rule the world are mostly satanically inspired. They distort, subvert, and pervert God's principles of government, health, culture, and education.

The city to which we belong has its foundations built by God. (Heb. 11:10.) Jesus said His Kingdom was not of this world's systems. He has an entirely different rule. The Kingdom to which we belong is of a different nature than those of the world.

> Jesus answered, "My kingdom is not of this world. If My Kingdom were of this world, My servants would fight, so that I should not be delivered to the Jews; but now My kingdom is not from here."
> John 18:36

We are not to be conformed to this world, but we are to be transformed by the renewing of our minds, that we may prove what is good, acceptable and the perfect will of God. (see Rom. 12:2.)

So if you wish to have a losing attitude, keep on acting, living, and thinking like the world.

Number Four: Hurtful to Others

The fourth losing position is to be hurtful to other people. There are people who deliberately hurt others. They say things to wound others on purpose. We need to get a new attitude, take a new position. We should establish firmly in our minds that we will not hurt others, if possible.

There are a lot of things you can say without talking about other people. Talk about the weather: it changes all the time. Talk about anything, but just leave people alone.

You would be surprised at the number of people who write me — hundreds, not just a few — asking me to straighten out the Church and the world. Some even write to straighten me out.

Concerning the Jim Bakker situation and the Jimmy Swaggart scandal, they wrote, "Why don't you step in there and do something about these things?"

The reason I have not is that, when I prayed about those things and the effect they were having on the Church world, the Lord told me to keep my mouth shut and my heart open and to pray for those people! And that is what I have done.

Those people who did a lot of talking did not help anyone very much, but prayer any time and any place always helps.

It is not my business to go through life hurting people. That is not my business. My business is healing people and changing people. That also needs to be your business.

Let's not have that hurtful attitude, that critical and judgmental spirit, that hurts others. Ephesians 4:32 says it so well: **Be kind to one another, tenderhearted, forgiving one another, just as God in Christ also forgave you.**

Number Five: Fearful

If we are fearful, that attitude haunts us. We are afraid of yesterday. We cannot let the past be the past. We are afraid of today, because we do not know what to do. We are afraid of tomorrow. It is coming for sure, and we do not know what to do about it.

God did not create man with a spirit of fear, and certainly, when you are born again, fear is not part of the new nature. **For God has not given us a spirit of fear, but of power and of love and of a sound mind** (2 Tim. 1:7).

Just say, "Fear, go. Fear, go, in the name of Jesus."

The Bible says fear has torment, (1 John 4:18) and you do not have to be tormented by fear. You will be a loser if you have fear on the inside of you and blame it on all kinds of other things.

Number Six: Unforgiveness

You have to forgive in order to win. You have to learn to let go of things that happen to you. What is more important than things happening to you is what you do about them. You can choose to turn loose of hurts and reactions.

If someone has cheated you, you must just say, "Well, you've added to my education. I had to pay for it, of course, but I have learned a lesson through this."

Education is sometimes expensive.

But you need to get unforgiveness out of your system, or it will clog your arteries of compassion. Unforgiveness will hinder militant love, and it will circumvent victory.

I have met people whose parents are dead, yet they still hate their parents. That is like hating a tree after the fruit is gone. Hate is wrong to begin with. Whether the person you are holding something against is living or dead, you have to get hate out of you.

Forgiveness is for your benefit. Most of the time, holding unforgiveness against someone does not hurt that person. However, it affects your mental, emotional, physical, and spiritual health.

Loose those people, and let them go. Forgiveness involves forgetting. Forgive and forget, and get on with living for Jesus.

Number Seven: Being an Obstructionist

There are homes where some family members want to lift one another up, but others are obstructionists. They keep their families held down. There are churches where three or four deacons who never had anything in their lives want to keep God's people from having anything.

When any repairs are needed, they say, "We can stand this another year."

If someone suggests having a revival, they say, "Oh, we couldn't pay for that!"

Be a helper when good things are suggested. Do not be an obstructionist. See how you can help, not how you can hinder. Do not try to find reasons why you should not do something. Find several reasons why you should have done it yesterday.

The Bible cautions against hindering the Gospel of Christ (see 1 Cor. 9:12). Rather, what we do, do it heartily, **And whatever you do, do it heartily, as to the Lord and not to men** (Col. 3:23).

13
Moses, a Militant Man

In the first chapter of this book, you read of the heroes of faith listed in Hebrews 11. Every one of those listed by the author of Hebrews — men and women — were militant people for God.

One of those men was Moses. Now Moses did not begin as a spiritually militant man. He spent the first two phases, or periods, of his life basically ignorant of the true ways of God. Yet, through faith, during his last forty-year period, he became a towering leader of God.

Very few people are remembered more than a decade. Fifty, or even a hundred years, is a long period to be remembered in history. Not many achieve lasting fame or a permanent place in man's remembrance.

However, Moses became a man of the millenia, a man remembered for thousands of years.

How did a man who acted on impulse, then retired to the backside of the desert for forty years in fear, change into a leader of millions of people? The thing that changed him was his developing faith that God was Who He said He was and would do what He said He would do.

He came to know that God really exists, and once he did, Moses moved out in a militant way.

All of the faith heroes are "action people:"

Abel offered, Enoch walked with God, Noah built an ark, Abraham left the land of his fathers and went to the land promised him. Go back and read the entire eleventh chapter of Hebrews in your Bible.

Can you see that God is trying to get your attention?

Militant People Overcome

Moses was born with two handicaps: He was a boy when all Israelite boy babies had been sentenced to death, and he was born a slave. It did not matter how he felt about freedom, he was not free. His parents, both of the tribe of Levi, made clay bricks for the Egyptian government. They were slaves; therefore, Moses was born into slavery.

His life shows, however, that you do not have to be a slave to your handicap. It does not matter if you were born in a poverty-stricken area, or born of parents hooked on addictive substances, or born with a physical handicap. Those things are not your destiny. You are your own destiny.

Many others in his situation gave up, thinking, "There's nothing I can do. I'm just one person. It's hopeless."

However, Moses had some advantages: His parents had faith, determination, and ingenuity. His father, Amram, declared that his son would not die at the hands of Pharoah. Moses' mother, Jochebed, and his sister, Miriam, "hid" Moses right out in plain sight.

After he was three months old, they strategically placed him where Pharaoh's daughter could not help but see him. You know the story. Pharaoh's daughter did see him and adopted him but allowed his mother to raise him for her until he was school age. Then for the rest of his first forty years, he lived the life of a king's son.

He learned the wisdom of Egypt, and Jewish writings tell us he was a mighty warrior-general in Pharaoh's army, even conquering Ethiopia. The only knowledge he had of the Israelites' history was from his parents.

I call that first forty-year period "the body life." In a sense, he lived a life of the flesh. Then, in the heat of indignation at seeing his own people, the Israelites, set at hard labor and mistreated, he killed an Egyptian overseer and had to run for his life.

Militancy: Body, Soul and Spirit

Phase two of Moses' life, the soul period, began when he fled to the desert. However, as soon as he arrived there, he found a lovely girl. She was one of seven daughters of a priest of Midian, which stretched from Ethiopia to the Mediterranean Sea.

Moses found her the same way several other Bible heroes found their wives — by going to the community well at the time of watering of flocks. It was the job of the young girls to draw water for the flocks, so it was a good place to see all of the marriageable girls of the area at one time.

As it happened, when Moses came up to the well, he found some ruffians trying to take the water away from Zipporah, and he ran them off. Of course, he was invited to her home and eventually married her.

Then he took over the job of caring for the sheep. That was his second phase of life for forty years. During that time, he had plenty of time to think his own thoughts. God only spoke to him once in forty years. That was the life of the soul, the life of the mind.

For forty years he could look into the limitless expanse of the heavens and think, "Who made you, stars? Why do you move a little each night? Why do I see you here and later there?"

Moses, according to Jewish writings, had a tremendous mind. Already, he had received the best education Egypt could offer. He had traveled, and probably, he knew as much about the world as anyone of his day. Yet, for forty years, all he did was spend time with his family, his wife's relatives, and tend sheep.

For forty years, the mental life developed in Moses.

I am sure there were times when he thought, "Lord God of my ancestors, God of Abraham, Isaac, and Jacob, who are You? Where are You now? You are the God of Isaac, who planted in the time of drought and had a hundredfold return. I would like to know You. What about my people, who You called Your people? They are still down there in Egypt suffering while I am living a peaceful, pastoral life up here in the desert country."

Then one day, he saw a bush burning with a fire that was not consuming it. I have been in the Middle East and have seen thousands of those desert bushes, and they burn quickly.

I am sure Moses thought, "That's funny. A fire that does not burn up a bush? I'll go over and investigate."

Then Jehovah spoke to him from the middle of the bush, the first recorded time the Lord ever spoke to Moses.

He said, . . ."**Do not draw near this place. Take your sandals off your feet, for the place where you stand is holy ground.**"

Moreover, He said, "**I am the God of your father — the God of Abraham, the God of Isaac, and the God of Jacob.**" **And Moses hid his face, for he was afraid to look upon God** (Ex. 3:5-6).

At that point, Moses still had no boldness toward God, but God was about to bring him into a militant attitude. Read the rest of the story in Exodus to see the development of boldness and courage in Moses, so that he would speak forth the words of the Lord.

Moses' militant attitude in the body life (carnal) only led to murder. His attack on the overseer was not Spirit-led, but was an impulse born of anger. Then he retreated into the life of the mind, into soul life. You are a spirit, who has a soul (personality — mind, will, emotions), and who lives in a body (a "suit" designed by God to move and function in the natural world and to house the real person, who is a spirit). Mankind is a race of spirits made in the image of the Living God, the Creator, who is spirit made of supernatural materials.

Every human whose body dies walks out of it to live eternally in heaven or hell. Everyone has eternal life, because everyone is spirit, made of eternal substances. The only question is where you will live eternally. The body, the "suit," decays and goes back into the elements of the earth. However, the person never ceases to live.

True Militancy Is of the Spirit

When Jehovah first commissioned Moses, he did what many of us do: He argued with God. He told the Lord all the reasons why he could not do what the Lord wanted. Here is the Creator of the universe, and Moses says He does not know what He is doing. God has made a mistake. Does that not sound like us?

God said to Moses, "What is that in your hand?" (Ex. 4:2).

That is what God always says to you when you argue with Him. Then, if you will let Him, He always shows you what you can do with what is in your hand.

Finally, after a long conversation and several more arguments which God firmly answered, Moses submitted and started off to live his third forty years — the life of the spirit man.

Did you know the greatest lawgiver in the world was born that day? Six hundred and fifty laws he inscribed for a nation. No one man has ever laid down that many laws single-handedly.

He is the greatest miracle-worker in terms of numbers that the world has any record of. Jesus' miracles and healings that are recorded amount to about thirty-four. Moses is recorded as doing forty-six.

Jesus did many more things than are written, as John said, however, I am simply talking in terms of recorded miracles.

> **And there are also many other things that Jesus did, which if they were written one by one, I suppose that even the world itself could not contain the books that would be written. Amen.**
>
> **John 21:25**

When Moses got out of the flesh, out of the soul, and into the spirit, he became a new man. And so will you. Becoming militant for God requires that you do not operate out of the body or the soul. You cannot be militant unless you also are a man under authority, which means you cannot give orders unless you know how to take them from the Lord. Demons will laugh at you, if the real you is in rebellion against the Holy Spirit, or if your body and mind rule you. If things of the flesh rule you, you will not have spiritual authority.

Moses never would have been able to bring the Israelites out of bondage if he had not brought himself out of bondage first by submitting to God and becoming obedient.

Forty years is a lifetime. David was king for forty years, Solomon was king for forty years, and many of the judges ruled for forty years. But most of the time in the later years of Israel and on into our time, forty years is considered the length of a generation. That is the equivalent of three lifetimes that Moses lived.

His first "generation" was lived in a king's palace. He could have remained there and be known today as something like Nicho Nicho III and buried in one of those pyramids in a gold mummy case.

People would say, "What did he do?"

And all of the archaeologists would have to say, "We don't know."

Militancy Accomplishes the Lord's Purpose

Moses would not have been remembered as doing anything worthwhile in the flesh. But he did not live all of his life after the flesh. He did not live all of his life after the soul. Many millions of Christians still live by their emotions or by their mental programs. They have neglected to "put off the old nature" in favor of the new (Eph. 4:24). You will never be able to be truly militant unless you do.

The most exciting part of Moses' life really occurred toward the end of his life, when he called all of the people together and reviewed the wilderness years for them. The entire book of Deuteronomy is Moses' "deathbed speech." In it, Moses' walk for God as leader of Israel is made plain.

He came down to the end of his life able to say he had accomplished the Lord's purposes.

I had a dream once in which the Lord spoke to me and said, "I am going to let you live as long as you have a lot of work to do."

That means I may live forever, because I am not going to run out of work! I am going to look for it!

People say, "Aren't you busy?" and I answer, "Not as busy as I'm going to be."

The Apostle Paul wrote that he had **fought the good fight,** [and] **finished the race,** he had, **kept the**

faith (2 Tim. 4:7). To be honest, not many Christians finish their courses or run their races. They fall by the wayside. There are other thousands who backslide. It is more important to finish your course than to begin your course.

Moses said, "Not only have I finished the job of leading this people to where they can see the Promised Land, but I also have kept the faith. I have kept the faith."

I have promised God that, whatever other Christians do, I am going to keep the faith. I am going to keep my faith young and crisp. I am going to keep my faith vibrant and alive.

I am not going to say, "Well, I have preached fifty years. That is all I am going to give God."

No, I am going to give God the last breath I have. I am going to resist the devil to the last hour I live.

I want to die in action somewhere saying, "If you do not come to Jesus, you are going to hell."

That is the only message that is worth preaching on the face of the earth. Jesus is the door. You have only to pass through Him to go to Heaven, and He is not willing that any should perish.

Moses wrote down the history of the Israelites and the story of his own life. He wrote what we know as the Pentateuch, the first five books of the Bible.

But the moment came when he called all of the people together and said, "I am ready to go to heaven. I will appoint my successor, and I will lay my hands upon him. You obey him, and he will lead you a step farther in God."

Moses told the people, **"Be strong and of good courage, do not fear nor be afraid. . .; for the Lord your God, He is the One who goes with you. He will not leave you nor forsake you"** (Deut. 31:6).

Moses laid his hands on Joshua and imparted the holy anointing that God had placed on his own life.

> **Then Moses called Joshua and said to him in the sight of all Israel, "Be strong and of good courage, for you must go with this people to the land which the Lord has sworn to their fathers to give them, and you shall cause them to inherit it.**
>
> **"And the Lord, He is the one who goes before you. He will be with you, He will not leave you nor forsake you; do not fear nor be dismayed."**
>
> **Deuteronomy 31:7,8**

Then this great giant of God waved farewell to those masses of people and said, "I am going to climb a mountain."

Moses did not die in the flames. He did not die in the wilderness. He climbed a mountain. I have been to that mountain, and I have looked all over, because the Bible says the devil tried to find his burying place. The devil wanted to steal his bones. If the devil would steal bones, no wonder he is after live humans! In the book of Jude, the writer said that Michael the archangel, contended with the devil, **when he disputed about the body of Moses** (Jude 9). No telling what kind of battles angels fight to keep the devil away from our living flesh.

The man of faith climbed that mountain alone. We love our families, and we love other people. We may have great relationships and fellowship with others, but when each of us goes to meet God, we will go alone. Moses climbed that mountain at one hundred and twenty years old in his own strength.

Once he got to the top, he looked out to see the whole of the Promised Land from Mount Nebo. I have done the same thing. I have stood right there and looked out over the land.

Then God said, "Well, that's enough now. Lie down, Moses, and come home. I'll take care of your body. Just lie down, and come out of your body."

And it was all finished. God took care of the funeral for him and buried him. Here was a man who lived in three worlds — body, soul, and spirit. But he died a victorious winner for God after living a militant life for forty years.

God wants every one of His children to be like that. He wants you and me, at the end of our lives, to be like Moses. He wants us to be victorious militant warriors who hand over the treasures He has loaned us into the hands of younger people. Then we can walk with Him to the top of the mountain and go home to heaven winners.

Be a Moses!

14
More Than Conquerors

We are to know victory in our Christian walk. We are to be more than conquerors. Satan should be running from us, not after us. We have been delivered from the devil's snare. We are not to be captives of the evil one.

Everyone of those statements is grounded in the Bible.

Victory: The Christian's Assurance

The sting of death is sin, and the strength of sin is the law.

But thanks be to God, who gives us the victory through our Lord Jesus Christ.

1 Corinthians 15:56,57

Victory Over the World

For whatever is born of God overcomes the world. And this is the victory that has overcome the world — our faith.

1 John 5:4

More Than Conquerors

Who shall separate us from the love of Christ? Shall tribulation, or distress, or persecution, or famine, or nakedness, or peril, or sword?

... Yet in all these things we are more than conquerors through Him who loved us.

Romans 8:35,37

Courage To Conquer

[Jesus speaking:] **These things I have spoken to you, that in Me you may have peace. In the world you have tribulation, but take courage; I have overcome the world**

John 16:33 NAS

To be "more than conquerors" means significant and decisive victory. It implies offensive warfare, capturing and gaining ground, rather than merely winning a battle. It means making great progress, possessing and taking what belongs to you as a child of the King. It speaks of ruling and reigning, not just holding ground.

Satan on the Run

The Apostle Paul speaks of the Father qualifying us to be **partakers of the inheritance of the saints in the light** (Col. 1:12), who **has delivered us from the power of darkness and translated us into the kingdom of the Son of His love** (v. 13).

This implies that Satan, that "power of darkness," has been put on the run. That future inheritance will come because already in this life we have been found to be qualified soldiers, worthy of being delivered from the kingdom of Satan. Satan has been put to rout, demoralized and defeated.

Delivered From the Devil's Snare

Paul warns that there will be and are some who need **to recover themselves out of the snare of the devil, who are taken captive by him at his will** (2 Tim. 2:26 KJV). The idea is that they will come to their senses so they can escape from the trap and snare of the devil.

The devil is a dark and sinister foe dedicated to the damnation of humanity. The Apostle Peter warned that we are to be sober, self-controlled and alert, because our enemy, the devil prowls around like a roaring lion looking for someone to devour. We are to resist him with strong and firm faith. (See 1 Pet. 5:8,9.)

There are many Old Testament references to the word *snare;* it was a word in common use. One of the best-known references is to be found in Psalm 91 which is a favorite of many. It goes like this:

> **He who dwells in the secret place of the Most High shall abide under the shadow of the Almighty.**
>
> **I will say of the Lord, "He is my refuge and my fortress; My God in Him I will trust."**
>
> **Surely He shall deliver you from the snare of the fowler and from the perilous pestilence ...** (vv. 1-3).

I heard of a young man who claimed these verses as his when he went into military service. He felt that they brought him through combat safely.

This psalm actually is a messianic psalm. It was a psalm known by Satan. He used it when tempting Jesus. The psalm goes on to say **For He shall give His angels charge over you, to keep you in all your ways. They shall bear you up in their hands, Lest you dash your foot against a stone** (vv. 11,12).

Jesus knew how to rout Satan, and He knew how to keep from getting trapped in the "fowler's snare." This was hand-to-hand kind of spiritual warfare, combat that was very real to the Son of God. When the devil tempted Jesus, He said, **Get thee behind me, Satan ...** (Luke 4:8a KJV)

This example is for our benefit as we engage in spiritual warfare with the enemy of our souls. To be delivered from devilish snares is to accept God's way of deliverance and victory.

Protection Against the Enemy

The prophet Isaiah prophesied that no weapon formed against God's own would prosper. This, he said, is "the heritage of the godly" (see Is. 54:17). This makes us more than conquerors. This means everything that Satan flings against us won't work. In the original Hebrew, this Isaiah verse is translated as: "No plan, no instrument of destruction, no satanic artillery shall push you or run over you, but it will be done away with."

This is God's promise that He will protect His own against Satan's attacks. The reward for militant Christians is the privilege of becoming more than conquerors.

Where there is righteousness in the heart, there is peace.

> **In righteousness you shall be established; You shall be far from oppression, for you shall not fear; And from terror, for it shall not come near you.**
>
> **Whoever assembles against you shall fall ....**
> **Isaiah 54:14,15b**

In World War II, we relied on our allies and they relied on us. It was mutually beneficial. We needed each other. Just so, while our adversary may be great, our Ally is much more powerful. The Holy Spirit can be depended upon to provide the help and power we need. The promise is, **Faithful is He who calls you, and He also will bring it to pass** (1 Thess. 5:24 NAS).

Overcomers Are Destined To Rule With Him

It is clear throughout history and the Bible that God's ultimate destiny for His children is that they rule with His Son. Overcomers are destined to rule with him: **To him who overcomes I will grant to sit with Me on My throne, as I also overcame and sat down with My Father on His throne. He who has an ear, let him hear what the Spirit says ...** (Rev. 3:21,22).

15

Forcefully Advancing
and Fighting for the Kingdom

And from the days of John the Baptist until the present time the kingdom of heaven has endured violent assault, and violent men seize it by force [as a precious prize] — a share in the heavenly kingdom is sought for with most ardent zeal and intense exertion.

Matthew 11:12 AMP

It was Jesus who said that beginning with John the Baptist, the kingdom of heaven has endured violent assault and that it would continue until the day the likes of John are taken into the Kingdom.

John lost his head for the sake of the Gospel. Stephen was stoned a little later. It was a time of violent assault against righteousness. Early Christians fled for their lives. The blood of the saints was spilled as Christianization of the Roman Empire took place. The record of Imperial persecutions has gone down in history as a bloody, violent time. Thousands were slain when they refused to give up their beliefs.

There was a time when Christians had become so numerous in Asia Minor that the heathen temples were almost forsaken. Imagine that!

But the persecution and torture of Christians was cruel and barbarous, with thousands being thrown to wild beasts in the arenas with spectators cheering; or they were crucified, burned, beheaded, or used as human torches. Those who were tortured for their faith endured without flinching. Multitudes perished in Rome, North Africa, Egypt, Asia Minor. One historian wrote: "The whole world is devastated."

It was a resolute, determined, systematic effort to abolish the Christian name. In the catacombs of Rome there exists vast subterranean galleries, commonly 8 to 10 feet wide, 4-6 feet high, extending for hundreds of miles beneath the city. They were used by Christians as places for refuge, worship and burial in the Imperial persecutions. The number of graves of Christians are estimated at being between 2,000,000 and 7,000,000.

And it had its beginning, Jesus said, when John began to preach holiness. That will get things stirred up all right.

If there is going to be a "Kingdom of God," we will have to fight for it.

Peace by Violence

When I was a boy, we had a bully in our school. (You probably experienced that also, most schools do!) I couldn't go to school peaceably. This guy would hit, push and shove me for no reason. I was scared spitless. Scared to even open my mouth. But I never squealed on the kid either at home or at school. I just endured it.

One day as we were walking along, this bully was not only teasing me, but others, too. I said to myself, "If he's on the street and I'm on the sidewalk, we are about the same size," and before you know it, that made sense in my head and I grabbed the kid's shirt, pulled him close to me, and pushed him to the street level. I beat his nose flat until there was blood. They finally had to grab me off him. He never touched me after that. So much for the big bully!

The remarkable thing about the incident was that the kid didn't get mad about it and he never bullied me around again. I found out that peace came by violence.

We had peace after that. Are you aware that the devil doesn't understand any other kind of language? He only understands those who defeat him. The devil has no mercy.

Sin is that way. Jesus said that it is those who are ardently zealous and who intensively exert themselves who will get to crowd into the kingdom. Fight for it, is what Jesus was saying. Don't just sit around moaning, groaning and complaining about how bad the world is.

Biblical Violence Not Uncommon

The word *violent* is mentioned 57 times in the Bible in 56 different verses. The Matthew 11:12 verse is the only place in the Bible where the word violent is mentioned twice. From Genesis to the end of the Bible you will find violence. From Adam and Eve's fall, right through to the present time, the kingdom of God and the forces of Satan have been contending.

There is the story, for instance, of Jacob whose name meant "the supplanter." Jacob wasn't liked. He stole the birthright from his brother; he deceived his own father and his Uncle Laban. Jacob deceived others many times. But then something got ahold of him. He ran off with his wives and the treasure that he had. And he found himself between a rock and a hard place with his Uncle in pursuit, and his brother advancing toward him.

What do you do when you are in a tough spot? Jacob remembered to pray at the brook called Jabok on the east side of the Jordan as he attempted to get over into Canaan land. I admit it's a strange story, but there it is in the Bible, the account of Jacob the strong man, the mean cowboy, wrestling with a man. (Gen. 32:22-31.) Jacob wouldn't let the man go until he blessed him. It was a violent struggle. When asked his name, he replied, "Jacob."

Then the man said, **Your name will no longer be Jacob, but Israel, because you have struggled with God and with men and have overcome** (v. 28 NIV).

Jacob came out of the struggle with a limp, the result of the socket of his hip being wrenched out of place. "This leg hurts, but I'm a changed man," he said to his family as he came back dragging his leg. "Hallelujah!" he shouted. "Now my name is Israel. Everything's right between God and me! Hallelujah! But I became violent last night. I wrestled . . . ."

How do you think his family reacted to that? "I wrestled with a man . . . I wouldn't let him go until he gave me heaven's blessing. I'm no longer Jacob; now I'm Israel."

Still disbelieving, his family looked at him in awe. "We'll call the place Peniel, it's because I saw God face to face, and yet my life was spared" (v. 30 NIV).

The name Jacob is in the Bible 358 times, but Jacob's new name, Israel, is in the Bible 2,565 times. That's what God can do with a nobody. That's what God can do for you if you fight for what you really ought to be. Jacob overcame and became a new man. God will do that for you also.

If you are a backslider, it's because you didn't resist and fight hard enough.

God Wants His Children To Be Winners

God wants His children to be winners. Look at Moses again — from the point of being killed to being raised in the king's palace; from killing a man to running for his life; from living on the backside of the desert to leading a vast host of people in the desert for 40 years. When he came to Egypt to get the Israelites out, he was fierce, a fighting man. He challenged Pharaoh through ten rounds, and in the last round the king's son was dead. "Get out of here," the king cried and Moses marched out more than a conqueror. He was a sure winner!

We have too many non-resisters in our churches today. Too many who are acquiescent. Too many who compromise their beliefs. Too many who are afraid, who keep their mouths shut in the presence of sin and sinners. Such are not included in that number whom Jesus said would share in the kingdom because they were willing to endure violent assault by fighting back with ardent zeal and intense exertion.

When we study the word of God, we see such remarkable things. There was David — David watching over his father's sheep. Calm little boy. Little shepherd boy composing the twenty-third Psalm. "The Lord is my shepherd ... " he mused as he watched those frolicking sheep.

Can you imagine it? An intelligent man talking to sheep. "Baaa, Baaa ..." Yes. I think those sheep understood this boy's spirit. "The Lord is my shepherd, I shall not want. He maketh me to lie down in green pastures: He leadeth me beside the still waters .." But those waters were soon to be disturbed. The moment came when a bear came. You can't compose psalms when a bear comes.

Some of you reading this would like tranquil waters and reciting the twenty-third Psalm for the rest of your days, but there are bears out there where you live too.

And the bear came. What did David do? "The violent take it by force ..." He jumped up and shouted, "You just made a mistake, bear. You made a big mistake bear," and he grabbed him by his whiskers, yanked him high in the air, busted his jaw wide open and by the power of God killed that bear. And then he had a new song. Another psalm to compose.

Some of you haven't killed a rabbit yet.

You've got to get into this thing. You've got to kill bears. Who are the big bad bears? The devil and his bunch who come to devour, take prey, and kill.

You've got to watch over one another. With love. Resisting the evil one. You're not to be a complacent Christian. On your way to the kingdom there is no free ride. Jesus said you crowd toward the kingdom of heaven by fighting the devil. It's violence all the way.

"The kingdom suffereth violence. . ." Jesus said. Pornography. Child molestation. Murder. Abortion. "Only the violent can withstand, forcefully advancing . . . ."

So you have to decide inside of yourself: "Am I going to lose the kingdom, or be numbered among those taking it?" God would like to put a militant spirit within you. He did it for David. He'll do it for you.

When Goliath, that enormous giant advanced toward David bellowing like a bull, cursing Jehovah, David had the courage to stand up against him. The runt of the family, without polished armor, said, "God gives me what I can fight with," and he took one look at that long-legged devil of a Goliath, let go with one well-aimed stone from his sling, and the cursing giant fell. "The kingdom of heaven suffereth violence, and the violent take it by force." David became king and the Bible tells us the rest of the story.

The name *David* is mentioned 1,085 times in the Bible. David was God's man just as you can be God's man or woman. And if you have to climb out of your family tree, do it to the glory of God. Be different from your family if that's what it takes.

History Records the Truth About Overcoming by Force

We can look back through history and see a man like Martin Luther. He was climbing the Scalasanta in Rome. I have been there. They say the wood of those steps from the ground floor up to the second floor, is from Jerusalem where Pilate stood and cried, "Behold, the man," as he looked at Jesus. But Martin Luther was climbing those until his knees bled, pleading forgiveness for his sins, doing penance. And halfway up those stairs, God spoke to him, and said, "Martin, the just shall live by faith."

And something filled Martin's heart. Joy. Peace. Warrior-spirit filled his heart. He was no longer a simple priest studying Hebrew and Greek. He came out of the Roman church, went back to Germany, and nailed his ninety-five thesis on the door of the church in Wittenberg, and all hell broke loose.

You can study the life of Martin Luther and the mistreatment he endured. But that man brought a great revelation to the whole of Europe and Europe came out of the Dark Ages igniting the spark that set it aflame.

He was lied about. Cursed. Reviled. His life endangered. Summoned by Charles V, Emperor of the Holy Roman Empire (which at that time included Germany, Spain, Netherlands and Austria), to appear before the Diet of Worms, and in the presence of the assembled dignitaries of the Empire and the Church, ordered to retract. He replied that he could retract nothing except what was disproved by Scripture or reason: "Here I stand; I can do naught else; so help me God." He was condemned, but he had too many friends among the German Princes for the edict to be carried out. He was hidden by a friend for about a year, and then returned to Wittenberg to continue his work of speaking and writing. Among other things he translated the Bible into German, thus bringing about the "spiritualization" of Germany. He was instrumental in starting the Protestant Reformation leading the world in its break for freedom from one of the most despotic periods of time in history.

Martin Luther was a conqueror; a winner who took the kingdom by violence. The Lutheran Church is still called by his name today. He was a fighter. And God would like for you and me to be the same against sin, rebellion and hatred of truth.

I could name many great men and women from the past who, like these we have looked at in this chapter, were unafraid to fight for what they believed. They knew that **Greater is he that is in you, than he that is in the world** (1 John 4:4 KJV).

Let us rise up together.

Winners never quit.